Montessori Architecture
A Design Instrument
for Schools

MW01091924

 PARK BOOKS

Montessori Architecture

Initially, Maria Montessori's educational method was intended for what we now refer to as 'neuro-diverse' children, to draw out and draw on their individual potential, but it was her brilliant idea to then apply this method to all children that ushered in the idea of a child-centred, more play-related approach to learning, paying special attention to when each child was most receptive.

This meant a break with established ideas on education. And it's easy to see that this other paradigm of the personal approach has considerable spatial consequences. This 'Design Instrument' is intended as a guide to those consequences. Thus, the classroom with its traditional military disposition of pupils opposite a teacher with the blackboard as the dominant focal point can cede to a more informal layout of tables formed into groups of those who want to sit together in a more homely ambience. With everyone's attention no longer fixed on one central figure but decentralised, as it were, the need arises for more varied places and an articulated space better suited to a differentiated organisational structure. At the same time, all pupils are engaged in doing work they choose themselves. In order to help them choose, it is vital that all possibilities are stripped of their complexity and offered as openly as possible, as if they were games. This requires that everything should have enough space to be laid out or otherwise disposed, meaning there should be thickness and depth, in other words volume. Amenities such as cloakroom corners, display cases, widened shelves above doors and on window frames, raised additional window ledges, built-on cupboards, study niches, window worktops, kitchen recesses or islands – all these see to it that everything gets its own recognisable place, establishing a degree of clarity in an otherwise dense fog of attributes and eventualities.

An environment that is to create the conditions for learning has to be able to accept the most varied contents within the intimacy of the place; learning requires that you have the whole world around you. Shelves, compartments, nooks, ledges and walls doubling as cupboards help you to frame things so that each acquires value in itself and will command attention, while at the same time there is clarity of organisation.

Montessori education wants a classroom to be like a living room and a school like a house – familiar territory, in other words. But our heterogeneous society requires that school is the place for preparing you to deal with other views and thus to question values. And there is no more receptive audience than children, for whom not everything is an undisputed fact. This is precisely why the school environment must above all be attuned to social relations and everything that can contribute to that end spatially must be seized on and given the focused attention of architects and designers. We are calling for a more open, accessible approach, with less detachment as exemplified by disconnected storeys and preferably grouped round a central hall where everyone can see everyone else. It must be full of places for unpremeditated encounters, where you can stop to talk, however briefly. A central hall acts as an urban square where pupils can converge, inciting a sense of community, a place where situations affecting everyone are shared. This makes the school a town as well as a house, where familiarity links arms with the challenges of otherness and the new.

You might assume that individual learning is incapable of inducing a feeling of community, but it is precisely this exchange among individuals able to think for themselves that can incite dialogue.

In spatial terms, it is essential that the cramped patterns of thought still often adhered to by school-builders should be abandoned in favour of more varied, more changeable and, most of all, more open space forms that incite greater concentration but also greater exchange, giving a more expansive view of the world. It is not enough to just simply demolish walls and leave large open areas where everyone is a bother to everyone else.

We are just going to have to accept the idea of another kind of school, one that is less of an institution where you are robbed of your freedom, if only temporarily, and fed with knowledge. We need to look for a form of learning spaces with a wider range of experiences, as is found in the city and in the world of the Internet.

The school for which we are to find a form is one of less education and more learning. What is needed is an environment that stimulates and incites learning by asking questions, a climate that provokes exchange and confrontation, intellectually, culturally and politically.

When study goes beyond the limits of so-called compulsory subject matter to become more extensive if not all-encompassing, learning is no longer restricted by the classroom walls but will claim the entire space of the building.

Montessori Architecture seeks to follow the ideas of Maria Montessori in space and form, but need not be construed as exclusively Montessorian. It is about all initiatives to reform the traditional school type, their common theme being the development of each child's capacities. The unwritten goal of traditional education, as we know, is to prepare children for a successful career in the world at large by giving them the necessary knowledge and understanding of the values, standards and information regarded as fact as the set of instructions they need in life. True individual learning can only be achieved by no longer regarding children generically as incomplete adults. Rather, asserting each child's own qualities and potentials where our principal aim ought to be to draw out those qualities and potentials rather than stuffing the developing brain with knowledge. Imparting knowledge is fine, but our first priority is learning to think.

Herman Hertzberger

Preface

01
Hilla Patell was Co-Director of Training and Schools at the Maria Montessori Training Organisation in London from 1962 to 1989 and was a long-serving member of AMI's Pedagogical & Training Groups. She was also President of AMI (ad-interim) from 2004–2005.

02
In 1921/1922 architects Ad Grimmon and Barend van den Niewen Amstel prepared sketch drawings for a Montessori school which were endorsed in Maria Montessori's own hand.

03
Alexander; Ishikawa; Silverstein. 1977

04
North American Montessori Teachers Association.

05
The *NAMTA Journal*, Vol. 30–2. 2005

The idea for *Montessori Architecture* was seeded by Hilla Patell [01] in the early 1990s, when she asked me if I thought it would be possible to list characteristics which were important factors in the design of the Montessori environment and mentioned a mythology to do with an octagonal plan form. My instinctive response was that a number of common characteristics would naturally occur, and we speculated in conversation on what they might be; but I was ambivalent about an octagonal plan form, little knowing that it had been generated by Maria Montessori's own discussions with architects seventy-five years earlier. [02]

Later I wrote a list of ten characteristics for Hilla, and I came to refer to these as *Montessori Patterns* in deference to *A Pattern Language,* the seminal work from 1977 by Professor Christopher Alexander and colleagues at the Center for Environmental Structure at Berkeley, California, USA [03] – which had been an important part of my years as an architectural student.

A discussion about *Montessori Architecture* had also been emerging in some of NAMTA's [04] publications under the editorship of David Kahn; following some interesting exchanges on the subject with David, he organised a symposium in 2005 at Taliesin West, Frank Lloyd Wright's campus in Scottsdale, Arizona, USA, with a small number of architectural students led by a young architect, Victor Sidy. David included me in the symposium which was constructed around the idea of 'Designing for a Montessori Continuum', the 'Montessori Continuum' being the concept of educational/developmental provision from birth to adulthood. It involved the Frank Lloyd Wright students in developing design schemes around principles derived from Montessori pedagogy for all ages and all Planes of Development, including university and adulthood. The symposium was an opportunity to test the idea of *Montessori Patterns* and happily some of the patterns emerged in the work presented by the students. [05]

The idea of specific *Montessori Patterns* has contributed to many discussions over the years and even to built projects in which I've been involved, notably at the Montessori Children's House in Hampstead, London, England and at the Corner of Hope Project, Nakuru, Kenya, and the idea seems to have withstood the test of time. When, in the course of this book project's development, we tested the idea against successful existing architectural projects around the world, we found that the patterns do seem to be there, readily identifiable. Given that Montessori pedagogy is derived from observation of the child's relationship with their environment and a key principle of the pedagogy is the idea of a Prepared Environment, I would argue that universal architectural patterns ought to be identifiable in every Montessori environment, be it a tent in the savannah or the thirty-fifth floor of a New York skyscraper.

06
Kramer. 1976

07
Published in English
as *The Montessori
Method*.

In 2015, the idea for *Montessori Architecture* took on a new dimension when, in discussions in Amsterdam with Soraya Lallani and Monika Arnold from the Swiss Arthur Waser Foundation, it seemed to correspond with an idea for preparing a set of modular blueprints for that foundation's Montessori projects in Tanzania. With global demand for Montessori schools growing exponentially, an imperative for sharing knowledge and experience in the making of Montessori environments had arisen. The board of the Arthur Waser Foundation was sensitive to this, and it committed to backing a *Montessori Architecture* publication project.

The project crystallised under the direction of Benjamin Stæhli alongside his work at the Arthur Waser Foundation and the Lucerne University of Applied Sciences. The schedule of patterns steadily expanded from the original ten to the twenty-eight published here. Benjamin brought to the project his knowledge of construction work with Ethiopian communities, and under his direction a prototype copy of this book has been used as a reference document for two architectural competitions in Tanzania. A winning competition entry is included in the repertoire section of this book.

At a certain moment, as work progressed, I learned from conversations with Joke Verheul and Carolina Montessori, at the Association Montessori Internationale (AMI) in Amsterdam, that Maria Montessori herself had had conversations with architects and designers about the nature of the Montessori environment. This ought to have been more obvious to me than it was, given the progressive circles Montessori moved in, but when news of a set of architectural drawings dating from 1922 emerged, it made me realise that any work on *Montessori Architecture* must be anchored in a context of Montessori's own engagement with architects and artists and possibly, furthermore, within the context of the milieu in which her work emerged. It's my view that, in the context of the broad sweep of art history, we might see Montessori not only as a pedagogue but also as a creator of important cultural artefacts and as the catalyst for the creation of the category of architecture which we identify in this book.

Montessori's own first experimental built project, a Casa dei Bambini or Children's House, created amidst the urban deprivation of Rome's San Lorenzo district, is well known. It opened on 6 January 1907 in the context of social upheaval and reform,[06] and it exists to this day. It was so successful that within just a few years this first Children's House had spawned countless copies across Italy, Europe and America.

Montessori's own observations in her Children's House provided material for her critically acclaimed book, *Il Método della Pedagogia Scientifica applicato all'educazione infantile nelle Casa dei Bambini*, which was published in 1909. It and its various translations[07] spread the message worldwide and, in consequence, the first Montessori school in the USA opened in 1911. By 1913 there were

08
Kramer. 1976

09
Montessori. 1913

10
Müller; Schneider. 2002

11
Montessori. 1967

12
Jansen. 2022

over 100 Montessori schools in the USA and Montessori spent a good deal of time there after delivering her first International Training Course in Rome in January 1913.[08/09]

Returning to war-torn Europe at the end of 1915 after her American lecture tours, Montessori chose Barcelona as her destination rather than Rome – she would not return to Italy until after the end of World War One. With Barcelona as the hub of an increasingly itinerant lifestyle, she would travel to London and Vienna (1919), Copenhagen (1929), Berlin, Paris and Rome (1930) and, interestingly for our story, to Amsterdam (1921, 1923, 1932), which along with Paris had emerged as a crucible of Modernism.

Model and experimental Montessori classrooms were opening everywhere. The first classroom in the Netherlands had opened in the Hague in 1914. In Cologne, in the same year, a fully equipped model Children's House was displayed by P. Johannes Müller, a German furniture manufacturer.[10]

In this climate of progressive thinking on education it was natural that state actors would be affected, and in 1917, along with the founding of the Netherlands Montessori Society, a critically important and progressive constitutional change was made by the Dutch whereby special education, in the sense of education based on the religious or philosophical convictions of parents and reflected in founding principles, was given equality with public education. Montessori education was recognised to be part of this group when Maria Montessori convinced the minister of education Mr De Visser that Montessori schools could not follow rigid timetables.

This change was seminal; it was the precursor to the passing into law of The School Act in 1920, which meant that special educational projects were assimilated into the public funding regime. State funding became the engine for a surge of progressive development focused on Amsterdam, and Montessori was invited to give a series of lectures at the University of Amsterdam in 1921.[11]

Amongst a number of new Montessori schools, a school within newly built premises at 157 De Lairessestraat on the margin of the Berlage urban development was planned, and Dutch architects Ad Grimmon and Barend van den Nieuwen Amstel were commissioned as designers. The director at the school was Rosalie Joosten-Chotzen, mother of Albert Joosten who would go on to become a Montessori pedagogue and author. Montessori visited the classroom every day for two weeks after it opened and it's possible that this is where she stayed when visiting Amsterdam to lecture in the succeeding years.[12]

Grimmon, an exponent of the Amsterdam School, particularly as an *architecte intérieure*, was working on exhibitions at the Stedelijk Museum and the Paleis voor Volksvlijt, with themes of social legislation and social benefit. He was also working on a number of schools for the municipality. Grimmon was sufficiently impressed with

13
This is described in the Ad Grimmon archive maintained online by Cilly Jansen: https://adgrimmon.nl/info

Fig. 01
Ad Grimmon and Barend van den Nieuwen Amstel. Circa 1921. *Watercolour drawings for the relationship between various spaces in a notional Montessori School.* Grimmon Archives; Cilly Jansen. Courtesy of Association Montessori Internationale

Montessori that he would prepare watercolour drawings of a notional Montessori school guided by Montessori herself. It's these drawings which are the likely source of the mythology of the octagonal plan form. It's also possible that they influenced the quatrefoil plan form of the Montessori school at Valkeveenselaan 21, Naarden, designed by Dutch architect Leendert van der Vlugt in 1925. The school is now a national monument in use as a residence.

The existence of Ad Grimmon's drawings might never have come to light except that in January 2014,[13] Cilly Jansen, Grimmon's great niece, discovered a suitcase in the attic of an Amsterdam antiquarian containing some of the watercolour drawings.

The watercolours reveal the detail of Montessori's engagement with Grimmon through her handwritten notes, plainly legible on the drawings, where she makes the following signed comment in Italian; 'This plan was made according to the idea of my method – in connection with the environment – and I think it is aesthetically excellent (especially the division into small spaces).'

Montessori's endorsement of the design itself, and particularly her interest in the division into small spaces, gives us an insight into her architectural thinking. The project, incorporating a domed octagon with apses, represents an important moment in the historical record. It creates an explicit connection with the foundational pattern used in our design tool which we call a 'Hierarchy of Interconnected Spaces'. It's a very progressive pattern, which we see time and time again in Montessori schools all over the world and it is paradigmatically in opposition to the institutional corridor and cellular classroom model.

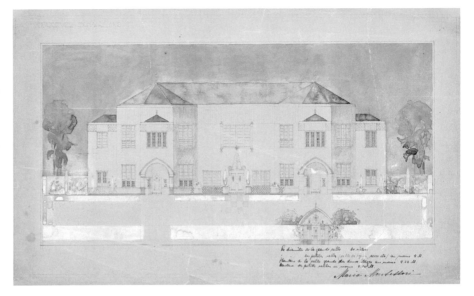

Grimmon's designs belong to Berlage's traditionalism and the Amsterdam School – the work is imbued with ideas of social reform but does
not engage with the radical aesthetic ideas also emerging in Paris and
Amsterdam, the ideas of Cubism, De Stijl and Modernism. Later, circa
1928, Grimmon would move towards Modernism.

      This time frame of radical ideas is the time frame of Mon-
tessori. Her idea for the deconstruction of the sensorial engagement of
the child into its component parts, her design of artefacts which, whilst
concrete, lead to the abstract, are the very ideas of Modernism.

      That Amsterdam was the crucible is not a coincidence;
it was inevitable. The same forces which shaped Modernism shaped
Montessori. The text in her books, the nature of the architecture emerging, the form, nature and colour of the material artefacts all indicate
a relationship with the mainstream of emerging Modernism.

14
Montessori. 1916

Fig. 04
Maria Montessori. 1916.
*Binomial Cube, contem-
porary manufacture.*
Nienhuis Montessori

If we explore the broad development phases of Montessori's material artefacts, we find four, each encompassing the development of materials, lecture courses and publications. There is a Rome phase from 1906 to 1913, an America-Barcelona-Amsterdam phase from 1913 to 1924, a Barcelona-London-Rome phase from 1924–1939 and an India phase from 1939 to 1948.

The Rome phase from 1906 to 1913 corresponds to observations in the Casa. She gives her first national training course in 1909, and the period culminates with her first international lecture in 1913. Innovation is driven by the demand created within a rapidly growing cohort of new schools opening throughout Europe and the USA. Montessori starts with material developed by Jean Marc Gaspard Itard and Edouard Séguin, then goes on to include Friedrich Froebel's material and her own original material. The period includes the publication of *Il Método della Pedagogia Scientifica applicato all'educazione infantile nelle Casa dei Bambini* and the preparation of *Dr. Montessori's Own Handbook*, published in New York and London in 1914, cataloguing her sensorial, practical life, mathematical and language material.

The America-Barcelona-Amsterdam phase finds Montessori in her late forties. It is an intensely productive period encompassing two lecture tours of the USA and includes the publication in 1916 of the Italian first edition of *The Advanced Montessori Method*, Volumes I and II. Volume II, extending to 455 pages, catalogues a wide range of grammar and mathematics material, much of it innovative and original. It's here for the first time we see listed Montessori's iconic binomial cube described thus:

The Cube of a Binomial: $(a+b)^3 = a^3+b^3 + 3a^2b + 3b^2a$.

Material: A cube with a 6 cm. edge, a cube with a 4 cm. edge; three prisms with a square base of 4 cm. on a side and 6 cm. high; three prisms with a square base of 6 cm. to a side and 4 cm. high. The 10 cm. cube can be made with these. These two combinations are in special cube-shaped boxes into which the 10 cm. cube fits exactly.[14]

15
Srinivasan; Ramachan-
dran; Srinivasan;
Roche; Venkatesan.
2009

16
Case 1914 No. 757
in the High Court of
Justice, Chancery Divi-
sion, London, relating
to infringement of
British Letters Patent
No. 06706 of 1912.

After 1924, Montessori's attention pivots back to Italy, where Musso-lini's interest leads to official recognition and government establish-ment of schools. However, Montessori remains domiciled in Barcelona with her son Mario, his wife and their four children. Mario, who trained in London in 1925, now contributes significantly to the development work and in 1934 *Psico-Geometría* and *Psico-Aritmética* are published in Spanish. These works catalogue this third phase of ever more de-tailed and complex material, including the geometry material and de-tails of a binomial cube conceived with glass prisms and coloured cubes, the trinomial cube as a natural extension of the binomial design, and the binomial cube's conceptual extension into additional dimen-sions along with designs for materialising the fourth and fifth powers. This period ends abruptly with the outbreak of the Spanish civil war and Montessori's rapid departure to London and then Amsterdam.

With Italy entering World War Two in 1940, Montessori, on a lecture tour of India with Mario, finds herself confined to the com-pound of the Theosophical Society [15] in Adyar, Madras (now Chennai). As a consequence, a fourth phase of material development occurs in India, encompassing botany material, a particular interest of Mario, and the development of ideas to do with young adult education, Earth stewardship and Cosmic Education.

It is clear that Montessori had a very determined attitude towards her intellectual property: she claimed ownership, she registered patents and she licensed a number of manufacturers to produce materials in return for royalty payments.

Her determinedly protective attitude is reflected in a 1914 court case in the Chancery Division of the High Court of Justice in London where Montessori, in conjunction with Philip & Tacey, her English licensee, sought to defend her Letters Patent 06706 of 1912. A company called Dawson Watson & Co. Ltd was advertising materials 'as used in the Montessori System' and Montessori sought an injunc-tion and damages. Whilst the action relating to the copying of the de-sign of 'Sandpaper Letters' and 'Proportion Material' was dropped in 1915, it indicates a strong desire for authenticity and control over the standard of manufacturing and materials employed.[16]

The effect of Maria Montessori's thinking on her cultural milieu was deep and profound, and I contend that it naturally extended into the realm of art and architecture. If we look at the coloured gra-dation and pairing tablets from the 1914 *Handbook*, we can see that they correspond with the colour theory teaching of Johannes Itten and Wassily Kandinsky at the Bauhaus. If we examine Kandinsky's 1931 *Sign Series*, it brings to mind Montessori's Grammar Material. Kandinsky's student analysis of the basic geometrical shapes at the Bauhaus reminds us of Montessori's Geometry Demonstration Tray. If we compare Montessori's Trinomial Cube with Piet Mondrian's 1920

Fig. 05
Johannes Itten. 1921.
*Colour Sphere in
7 Light Values and 12
Tones.* Museum of
Modern Art, New York;
c/o Pictoright
Amsterdam 2022

Fig. 06
Maria Montessori. 1912.
*Colour Box 3, con-
temporary manufacture,
7 Light Values and
9 Tones.* Nienhuis Mon-
tessori, Amsterdam

Composition with Yellow, Red, Black, Blue and Gray or Gerrit Rietveld's 1924 *Red and Blue Chair*, we are arrested by the comparison.

None of this is surprising: a core idea in Montessori's pedagogy is the chronological relationship between the concrete and the abstract in a child's exploration. Children work first by manipulating physical materials and progress into the abstract ideas which correspond to them.

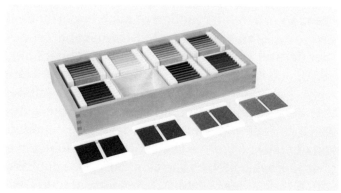

15

17
Montessori. 1914

18
Montessori. 1914

Fig. 07
Wassily Kandinsky.
1931. *Sign Series.*
Fondation Beyeler, Basel

In *Dr. Montessori's Own Handbook*, first published in 1914, Montessori says, in relation to the use of the number rods, 'When the figures are known, they will serve the very purpose in the abstract which the rods serve in the concrete; that is, they will stand for the uniting into one whole of a certain number of separate units.'[17]

On the wooden geometrical insets, she says: 'Again, the refinement of the eye's power of discrimination increases every time the child passes from one series of cards to the next, and by the time that he has reached the third series, he can see the relation between the wooden object, which he holds in his hand, and an outline drawing; that is, he can connect the concrete reality with an abstraction.'[18]

This is the idea at the heart of Modernism, that an abstraction can represent reality. Thus, in 1920, in Amsterdam, Montessori found herself in the midst of, and contributing to, an explosion of progressive ideas to do with social organisation, education, urban planning, art, architecture and literature. Her very presence in Amsterdam was itself a direct consequence of the far-sighted 1920 Primary Education Act which guaranteed state funding for progressive schools. Montessori arrived in Amsterdam as the Amsterdam School of de Klerk, van der Mey and Kramer was reaching its apogee in the Berlage Plan, an urban intervention of such importance that in 2018 it was given the status of 'protected townscape'. The Amsterdam School founders all worked for the Cuypers architectural bureau until about 1910, and it was also the starting place for Ad Grimmon's career.

Montessori's first schools in Amsterdam were part of that Berlage urban plan, but emerging in intellectual conflict with this was the avant-garde movement of De Stijl, founded by Mondrian, Bart van der Leck, Theo van Doesburg, Gerrit Rietveld et al. The first issue of its journal, edited by van Doesburg, was published in October 1917 with a radical manifesto.[19] Two years later, in Dessau, in April 1919,

Fig. 08
Theo van Doesburg.
1925. *Counter
Construction*. Collection
Stedelijk Museum,
Amsterdam

the Bauhaus School of Art was founded by Walter Gropius, which Kandinsky would join in 1921 and van Doesburg in 1922.

According to Theo van Doesburg in the introduction to De Stijl 1917 no. 1, the 'De Stijl' movement was a reaction to the 'Modern Baroque' of the Amsterdam School movement. Van Doesburg's 'Counter Construction' from 1925 captures the progress from the Amsterdam Style into Modernism.

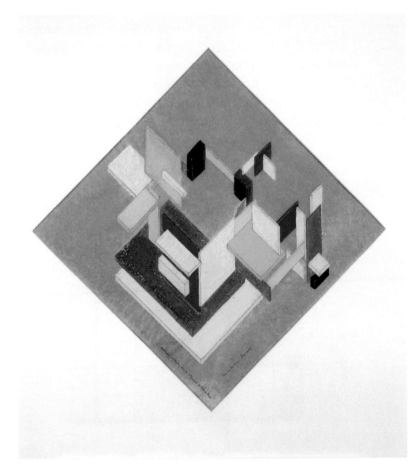

From 1914 to 1919, taking refuge from Paris and World War One, Piet Mondrian was resident in an artists' colony in the Dutch town of Laren. In Paris between 1911 and 1914, Mondrian's influences were Picasso and Braque and he described himself as a Cubist. However, during his time in Laren he encountered Bart van der Leck, Theo van Doesburg and mathematician and theosophist Mathieu Schoenmaekers, who exerted considerable influence. By 1917 Mondrian was describing his work as less pictorial but instead 'neoplastic'. The abstraction and use of primary colours for which he is principally known emerged during this period and the geometry he explored was catalysed by his exchanges with Schoenmaekers. Schoenmaekers, in his 1916 treatise *Beginselen der beeldende wiskunde* (Plastic Mathematics), describes a 'new plastic art' emerging from a 'new insight into relative objectivity'.

17

20
Sellon; Weber. 1992

21
Wilson. 1987

Mondrian had become associated with the Theosophical Society in 1909.[20] Theosophy is a thread which connects not only with Schoen-maekers but also with Maria Montessori, who had become a member in 1899, and others such as Wassily Kandinsky, Thomas Edison, who endorsed Montessori in the USA, Emily Lutyens, the wife of English architect Sir Edwin Lutyens with whom Montessori corresponded on the architecture of the Montessori school, and even Mahatma Gandhi who had briefly been a member whilst a law student in London in 1891.[21] An early masterpiece in Mondrian's neoplastic phase, *Composition with Yellow, Red, Black, Blue and Gray*, painted in 1920, signifies his emergence as an important influence in Modernism.

Another prominent influence during this progressive period is Gerrit Rietveld, the Dutch architect and furniture designer. Born in Utrecht, Rietveld became a member of De Stijl in 1919 and in 1924 he built the Rietveld Schröder House with Truus Schröder-Schräder, a progressive Dutch woman whose circle included the avant-garde artists and architects connected with the De Stijl movement.

Fig. 11
Gerrit Rietveld. 1924.
Red and Blue Chair.
c/o Pictoright
Amsterdam 2022

In 1917 Gerrit Rietveld designed his iconic red and blue chair. Early examples were not red and blue, however; the early versions in 1917 had neutral colours though by 1924, influenced by Bart van der Leck, the chair had been transformed into the red, blue, yellow and black primary-coloured and lacquered version we associate with Rietveld today. Precisely the same colour scheme as Montessori's iconic Trinomial and Binomial Cubes.

Rietveld's collaboration with Schröder-Schräder led in 1924 to the construction of the Rietveld Schröder House. Recently widowed and with three young children (her youngest daughter Han Schröder was born in 1918), Schröder-Schräder is likely to have been well informed on Montessori education. What we do know is that the Rietveld Schröder House, which still stands and is now a UNESCO World Heritage site, was used between 1933 and 1936 as a Montessori school.

We also know that Gerrit Rietveld designed a cabinet which was used in the Montessori school. It became known as the Montessori Cabinet and is in the archive of the Centraal Museum, Utrecht. A drawing of the cabinet, by Rietveld, which seems to have been used as a prototype for a range of furniture produced in 1936, is in the archive of the New Institute, Rotterdam (Museum for Architecture, Design and Digital Culture).

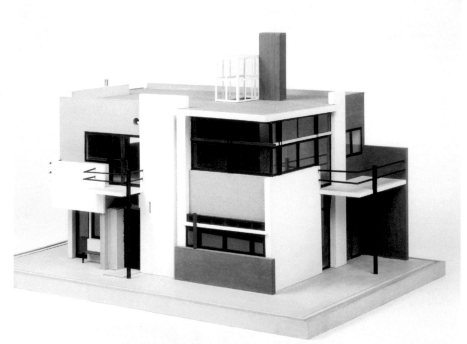

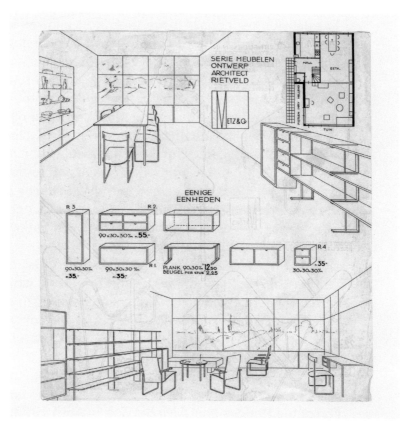

22
In an undated letter, but mostly likely from the early 1930s, Maria Montessori writes to an engineer and friend to say she has had a letter from Edwin Lutyens. She explains that on another occasion Lutyens had told her 'he would personally take care of the building of one of my "small houses" in London' and that he has now written to say that he has found a suitable site for it, near the Thames.

Fig. 14
Gerrit Thomas Rietveld. *Drawing of the Montessori Cabinet which became a prototype for a furniture collection produced by Metz & Co.* c/o Pictoright Amsterdam 2022

There is further archival evidence of Montessori's connection with progressive architects in an exchange of letters with Edwin Lutyens [22] in 1931. It's possible that this exchange was brought about as a consequence of a speech given by Mahatma Gandhi at the Maria Montessori Training College in London on 28 October 1931 at which Montessori was present. In 1931 Gandhi attended the Second Round Table Conference in London to decide on the future legal status of India. A law student in London in the 1890s, his legal training proved an asset in the conference negotiations. Lutyens had been responsible for the design of New Delhi as the new seat of the British Indian government from 1912 to 1930. What remains in the record certainly suggests that Montessori and Lutyens met and discussed the idea for a model Montessori school 'close to the Thames in London'. Lutyens, too, had a connection with the Theosophical Society – his wife Emily was a member and he worked on the architectural designs for the society's headquarters and temple in Tavistock Square, London, from 1911–14 and again from 1922–29; the building is now the headquarters of the British Medical Association.

Unfortunately, Lutyens's private archive of correspondence was destroyed in 1950–51 and so there is no record of any sketches or letters, and only Montessori's notes still exist. We can only speculate on what might have emerged from the meeting of these two extraordinary minds.

The development phase in wartime India allowed Maria Montessori's son Mario to come to the fore in terms of pedagogical development. This phase of collaboration with his mother, building on the vast design archive of materials already generated, turned to the opening out of the Montessori pedagogy for young adults and their relationship with the Earth. The time also allowed reflection on her legacy and preparation for the publication of several new books, including *Educazione e pace* (1949), a collection of lectures on education and peace. In 1946 Maria and Mario returned to Amsterdam and to the Association Montessori Internationale which had been protected by Ada Pierson during the war. Ada had also taken care of Mario's four children, by his first wife Helen Christy, during Mario's absence. Later, in 1947, Ada and Mario married.

The Association Montessori Internationale had been founded during the first Montessori Congress, which was part of the Fifth Conference of the New Education Fellowship at Kronborg Castle, Helsingør, Denmark, in 1929. Present at the conference were important pedagogues such as Jean Piaget, Helen Parkhurst, Pierre Bovet and Paul Geheeb.

AMI was later, formally and legally, constituted in Berlin in 1932 but, following the introduction of 'The Law for the Restoration of the Professional Civil Service' in April 1933, an extremely hostile environment towards the Montessori movement was 'endorsed'. Schools were closed and manufacturing of materials ceased, so AMI was relocated first to Barcelona and then, after 1935, as the clouds of civil war in Spain gathered, to Amsterdam, firstly to 22 Quinten Massijsstraat and later to 53 Michelangelostraat, both within the Berlage Plan. Following Maria Montessori's arrival in Amsterdam in 1946, a house in Koninginneweg, 300 metres from the De Lairessestraat school, was purchased as her home and to become the headquarters of AMI. It has come to be known as 'The Montessori House'.

Steve Lawrence

Montessori pedagogy

23

01
Annette Haines,
spokesperson
for Montessori Values,
Scholarship and
Research.

Montessori pedagogy considers education to be much more than the transmission of knowledge. It sees education as an aid to life, with its purpose the formation of the total personality. Humankind is neither more nor less than the sum total of all those individual personalities; thus, the child we must have in mind is, in a literal sense, the maker of tomorrow's society and will become tomorrow's custodian of the Earth's ecology. How will such a child be able to grow into that responsibility without an appropriate environment to adapt to in the first place?

It is in this context that we must consider the importance of the design of the Montessori environment. To do that we need to understand how Montessori pedagogy views the developmental trajectory of the human child, and the child's evident characteristics and tendencies.

'Thinking about human development permeates human history. The fact of development appears before our eyes with the birth and growth of every baby, yet we cannot help but wonder about the details. These details are endlessly fascinating because of the variance in human development and the variance in human cultures. The human mind searches for the simplest theory of human development that explains the variance, generalizing over all differences in culture and time. Furthermore, this simple theory should allow for the description of optimal human development, encompassing both philosophical and psychological elements.' [01]

The requirements placed on the architectural environment are obviously quite different for an infant or a young adult; they are, however, on a continuum with some *Montessori Architectural Patterns* applicable across the whole continuum, and some are quite specific to an age range. It is natural that children closer to adulthood require an environment closer to the everyday adult environment and therefore the *Montessori Architectural Patterns* we describe are biased towards younger ages and particularly the three-to-six age group. This is the seed age group for most schools and these patterns are known as the Children's House. A demand to provide educational environments for children aged zero to three and six to twelve will often be a natural consequence of the pre-existence of the Children's House. The very phrase Children's House or Casa dei Bambini puts us in mind of an architecture which is different from that of the Adults' House.

Montessori pedagogy identifies what it refers to as 'Four Planes' evident in children's development. These planes are broadly distinct chronological phases where different characteristics and needs are evident. We must naturally have these characteristics and needs in mind when considering the Montessori Prepared Environment and the *Montessori Patterns*.

Montessori pedagogy's Four Planes of Development are broadly: birth to six, six to puberty, puberty to eighteen and eighteen to adulthood, puberty being around the age of twelve and adulthood, as the biomechanical maturity of the organism, around the age of twenty-four. But the Four Planes are not simply chronological age groupings, they are distinct phases in the child's self-construction of their personality and in their adaptation to society and the world.

Maria Montessori used a delightfully simple but expressive chart to explain the idea of a trajectory through the 'Four Planes of Development' from birth to adulthood. She describes the emergence of the predominantly unconscious mind from birth to three, the dominantly conscious functioning mind from three to six, and the emergence of the self-reflective young adult between twelve and eighteen who evolves into a thoughtful contributing member of adult society between the ages of eighteen and twenty-four.

THE FOUR PLANES OF DEVELOPMENT

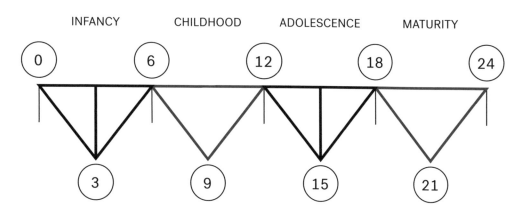

ESSENTIAL CHARACTERISTICS

Montessori pedagogy is designed to nurture the constructive instincts of human beings to create themselves (what Montessorians refer to as the universal Human Tendencies). These Human Tendencies are our guide in interpreting the *Montessori Patterns* and we can organise them into meeting social, moral, cognitive and emotional needs. If we can identify these constructive instincts and place them within the context of the constructive rhythm of life that we call the Four Planes of Development, then the architectural patterns identified become universally applicable, no matter the resources, culture, or prevailing prejudices of what constitutes supporting learning environments for children. We are primarily concerned here with the first three planes, the fourth occurring within what is essentially an adult domain, and which in the Montessori continuum is the university, the college of further education, apprenticeship studio, laboratory, ecological workplace and so on.

THE FIRST PLANE OF DEVELOPMENT:
BIRTH TO SIX

The First Plane of Development is divided into two roughly equal parts requiring particular environments to be designed for young infants and toddlers. For working parents, a 'Nido' is provided for non-walking infants. For all walking children, an 'Infant Community' is designed to accommodate the new capacities of the toddler. Environments are then redesigned for children of approximately three to six years of age in what is called the Children's House.

The baby's first environment is the mother, and orientation to the external world begins at birth. The sustaining mother's embrace is the place from which the impulse to relate to others emerges. Social adaptation occurs, at first, from the security of the mother's proximity and the infant environment accommodates the mother or carer in circumstances of security where trust and confidence can build. Babies everywhere will babble at around six months, walk at twelve months and talk at two years. In the period before three there is a huge growth in the urge to explore, to be independent, to seek out others, to engage in meaningful activity, to communicate and express an opinion, to orientate, to be creative, solve problems and invent solutions. The environment must necessarily be designed to accommodate this: it must allow freedom of movement, be resource-rich and provide access to sensorially rich activities that the children may use to progressively build their independence and explore the world in which they live.

When the child leaves the Infant Community and emerges into the Children's House, they move into a world that sustains their intellectual, psychological, social and emotional needs. The Children's House has resources for the children to be engaged in the activities of their daily life, it has activities that develop their sensory perceptions and link them to the real world for exploration. There are numerous activities for language development and the exploration of their cultural world, including mathematics, geography, history, biology, science, art, music, etc. The materials aid the development of executive functioning, a group of cognitive skills which allow the child to pay attention, plan and organise, to retain and recall information so that it can be used in learning and problem-solving.

In the Children's House the child acquires self-discipline (inhibitory control), builds working memory (concentration), and achieves cognitive flexibility (problem-solving). The paradigm is one of meaningful activities, freely chosen and freely available, within a built environment planned for maximum engagement with a multiplicity of challenges and with very little need for adult intervention.

For the designer this is extremely thought-provoking and requires an understanding of the range of materials, their relationships with each other, their dimensions and their storage needs, along with the increased autonomy of the children, their need to work individually but also in community, and the necessity to move beyond the physical confines of their classroom. The key ideas are driven by the human tendencies for movement, meaningful activity, work, independence, orientation, exploration, communication, order and precision.

THE SECOND PLANE OF DEVELOPMENT: SIX TO TWELVE

From a pedagogical point of view, the Second Plane of Development is a single plane. In practice, however, it will often take the built form of separate six-to-nine and nine-to-twelve classrooms. In most regions these tend to be called 'elementary' classrooms. For the designer there should be a continuum across the Second Plane, with adjacent spaces which allow for children to transition of their own free will and according to their interests and motivations.

In the First Plane of Development, whilst children are engaged in individuation, forming themselves and their personalities, they mostly work on their own, at individual tables or on the floor. In the Second Plane of Development the urge to collaborate arises. Its source is the strength of personality which allows for the contribution to the group. The children are no longer satisfied working alone; they need to work together, and the environment must accommodate this immense developmental change. The groups they form are small, interest-related, fluid, usually multi-aged and arranged by the children themselves. Children in the course of their day will connect with more than one group and may still work individually at other times during the day.

For children in the Second Plane, large tables and plenty of floor space for collaborative, long-term projects are essential. Tables and chairs must be available for children of different statures. Tables will be used in multiple combinations. Shelf and worktop space must be available for models and large displays. This age group must have plenty of space, including closed storage so that raw materials can be stored and projects and presentations, independently researched, can be displayed and shared. These children are completely involved in helping support the life of the school and should have access to a kitchen so that they are able to be directly involved not only in growing but also preparing food on a daily basis.

Second Plane children exhibit a great interest in, and are very sensitive to, moral issues. They need to explore the issues of right and wrong, fairness and unfairness. It's therefore essential that the entire Second Plane cohort can come together, possibly in theatre-like or staged settings, for large group discussions to take place. Second Plane children are no longer intellectually satisfied by a closed classroom environment. They need access to other parts of their school, to a library, a creative arts studio, a carpentry workshop, a pottery studio, perhaps a laboratory. They also need an outdoor environment for botanical studies. In this age group we also see the emerging need for access to the outside world beyond the school itself, with planned and collaborative visits elsewhere, but with purpose, to explore and further research more deeply information that relates to their work. Their studies are interdisciplinary and situated within a study of the history of the Earth and its peoples, the cosmos and its laws. Key ideas to hold in mind are: ever-expanding intellectual curiosity, group work and exploration of moral dilemmas.

THE THIRD PLANE OF DEVELOPMENT:
YOUNG ADULTHOOD

Following on from the self-confident elementary age child who has established their personality as an individual and then asserted themselves as a confident contributor to the group, we see in the young adult human being the emergence of a vulnerable stage where the child is moving into his or her adult body, both emotionally and physically.

In the First Plane, children become a member of their family, needing close family connections. In the Second Plane they move away from this need, experiencing a new urge to be part of a group. Young adults emerging from the Second Plane's straightforward membership of the group find themselves confronting their relationship to their group(s) as they experience the urge to try out different personas and different social interactions. This stage of development carries vulnerability to criticism and a high degree of sensitivity to the peer group. There is a need to be valued. The young adult environment should encompass the potential for productive economic enterprise alongside the contribution enterprise can make to the creation of capital. This might, for example, include the making of tools to enhance productivity, adapting the environment, or setting aside seeds from a crop harvest for the future. This encompassing of the natural economic cycle in a way which is meaningful to the young adult offers them the opportunity to contribute to the community and take individual responsibility, which is critical to their social emergence.

Building on the intellectual exploration of the Second Plane, these young adults are ready to take responsibility for their actions and base their enterprise and work on the contribution they can make to the health and well-being of the planet and its peoples. In keeping with the pedagogical principle of moving from the concrete to the abstract, engagement with, and contributions to, the concrete aspects of enterprise, capital, property, value and wealth in their community creates the foundation for the intellectual exploration of abstract concepts of economics and their relationship with society and a community's constitutional organisation.

Enterprise within the community also allows academic study itself to be rooted in the real world, with the enterprise creating the objects of study. The enterprise must be necessarily rooted in its wider community, as this will give rise to rural enterprise in rural areas and urban enterprise in urban areas. For example, in a rural area the Montessori young adult community may take the form of a small farm.

The young adult curriculum is built around the community's property and the personal and social exploration will encompass the expressive arts. Music, art, drama, theatre, debate and sport are all part of this life of togetherness. Class sizes for this age group tend to be small, interest-driven and relate to the life being lived in the setting. Small group discussions are a vehicle for developing ideas and the built environment must allow for this. Individual responsibility and academic independence are standard.

The key ideas are: the place of the individual in the peer group, interdependencies, opportunities for self-expression. The environment of the Third Plane, in all likelihood, isn't wholly centred around the school setting.

THE FOURTH PLANE OF DEVELOPMENT:
INTO ADULTHOOD

The Fourth Plane of Development is early adulthood, from post-eighteen years of age up until around the moment of maximum biomechanical capacity at about twenty-four. At the culmination of the Fourth Plane the human being can be considered to be fully formed, physically, intellectually, morally, cognitively and emotionally, totally prepared for life and at peak capability.

The environment for the Fourth Plane, in all likelihood, isn't the school setting; it may involve travel and exploration, it may be a professional setting, a volunteer setting, an apprenticeship setting, a further education setting, a research setting or a combination of these. For many young adults emerging from a Montessori twelve-to-eighteen setting, it will be conventional university or a college of further education or the world of enterprising work. In circumstances where a Fourth Plane environment is part of a Montessori continuum, it is likely to entail an expansion and development of the young adult environment with threads of real world productive economic activity woven in. It is essential that the Fourth Plane environment provides the possibility of looking at life from different perspectives. Key ideas for the Fourth Plane individual are: economically rewarded enterprise, giving back to society, sense of identity, reflection on career choice.

○ Mixes children of different ages within classes according to the Four Planes of Development and their subsets. First Plane 0–3 and 3–6; Second Plane 6–9 and 9–12; Third Plane 12–15 and 15–18, Fourth Plane 18–21 and 21–24. (See chart page 29.)

○ Meets every child at their developmental level, enabling them to advance at their own pace in each domain. Children learn alone, from each other or together in small groups.

○ Embraces peer modelling, peer-to-peer engagement and teaching.

○ Adults facilitate, guide and support each child using their knowledge of child development and their observation of the child and their interactions with the environment and their peers.

○ The adult understands that it is children who need to be the agents of their own learning and scaffolds help and interventions accordingly.

○ The instruction is individualised with cooperative learning in small groups as children advance in age.

○ Learning is self-directed (freely chosen within appropriate limits).

○ Children's experiences enable them to develop themselves and also contribute to the community, creating a balance between independence and interdependence.

○ Collaboration not competition; knowledge and learning not teaching and telling; exploration and discovery not teaching to the curriculum or test.

○ The environment has a simple, uncluttered aesthetic and is made from natural resources that are respected and cared for by the children.

○ It 'breathes' sustainability and conscious care of resources; it should reflect a sense of 'place' both geographically and culturally.

○ It enables all children to engage in taking care of it and develop a sense of ownership and responsibility towards it.

○ It is designed to allow children to mix freely with one other, to move between spaces safely, connecting children to each other, in multiple ways and to the external environment that they may also access at any time.

○ All activities and learning materials have a logical place and are kept in good order and are freely accessible to the children.

01
Baker. 2018

02
Haines. 1993

03
James. 1892

04
Montessori. 1949

GLOSSARY OF MONTESSORI TERMS

Montessori pedagogy uses terms very specifically and some of them may be open to misinterpretation or they may carry a weight of meaning from other spheres. A glossary of terms is therefore a helpful tool in the context of a design instrument for *Montessori Architecture*. The glossary we reproduce here was extracted from one prepared by Dr Annette Haines and is taken from the *AMI Journal 2017–18*,[01] a celebratory edition of her work, with some minor additions, deletions and editing.

TERMINOLOGY USED INSTEAD OF GRADES, CLASSES, FORMS OR YEAR GROUPS

Nido
A place for children from about two months until walking well (around the age of fifteen months).

Infant Community
A place for children from walking well (around the age of fifteen months to approximately two-and-a-half to three years of age.

Children's House
The English name for Montessori's Casa dei Bambini (Italian). A place for children from two-and-a-half to three years to about six. Everything necessary for optimal human development is included in a safe and secure environment.

Elementary
The name given to Montessori classes for children from six years of age to twelve. Children may be divided according to the planes of development into Lower Elementary (six to nine) and Upper Elementary (nine to twelve).

Young Adult
There are no specific names for the ages twelve to eighteen. Maria Montessori referred to these children as the *Erdkinder*, highlighting the importance for this age group to be connected to the land. In *Montessori Architecture* we prefer the term 'young adult' to 'adolescent'.

MONTESSORI TERMINOLOGY (ALPHABETICAL)

Absorbent Mind
A mind able to absorb knowledge quickly and effortlessly. Montessori said the child from birth to six years has an absorbent mind.

Adaptation
Related to the idea of an absorbent mind[02] is a special power of the young child that can be called the power of adaptation. This power is a process whereby the young child uses the environment to develop and, in so doing, becomes part of the environment. The young child absorbs the culture of their time and place, taking in all the spirit, the customs, the ambitions/aspirations and attitudes of a society – simply by living in that society.

Concentration
Recognising that 'the longer one does attend to a topic the more mastery of it one has,' the great American psychologist William James remarked: 'An education which should improve this faculty would be the education par excellence.'[03] Montessori, who knew of James, set out to do just that. She believed that if environments could be prepared with 'objects which correspond to ... formative tendencies'[04] the child's energy and interest would become focused on that aspect of the environment which corresponded to the developmental need.

Concrete to Abstract
A progression both logical and developmentally appropriate. The child is introduced first to a concrete material that embodies an abstract idea such as size or colour. Given hands-on experience, the child's mind grasps the idea inherent in the material and forms an abstraction. Only as the child develops are they gradually able to comprehend the same idea in symbolic form.

Creativity/Imagination
Imagination involves the forming of a mental concept of what is not actually present to the senses. Creativity is a product of the imagination and results from the mental recombining of imagined ideas in new and inventive ways.

31

05
Standing. 1957

06
Montessori. 1956

07
Weiner; Simpson. 1991

Both are dependent on mental imagery formed through sensorial experience.

Cycle of Activity

Children, when engaged in an activity which interests them, will repeat it many times and for no apparent reason, stopping suddenly only when the inner need which compelled them to the activity has been satisfied. To allow for the possibility of long and concentrated work cycles, the environment must be designed to enable children to complete cycles of activity. These cycles may be achieved individually through single activities or collaboratively through a series of activities.

DEVELOPMENT OF CHOICE AND SELF-REGULATION

The ability to will, or choose to do something with conscious intent, develops gradually during the first phase of life and is strengthened through practice. The Montessori environment offers many opportunities for the child to choose. Willpower, or self-control, results from the many little choices of daily life in a Montessori school.

Earth Stewardship

Care of the environment is central to Montessori education. From the earliest ages children are engaged in building a collaborative relationship between themselves and others, and themselves and their surroundings. The youngest children (fifteen months to six years) begin their commitment to the Earth through direct action: taking care of plants and flowers, growing and harvesting them. They take care of animals and begin to use all their senses to observe them and their language to name and classify them. As they get older (six to twelve) they study the geological and geographical development of the Earth and its place in the universe. They investigate the emergence of life – plants and animals from the very beginning (as we understand it) of our planetary existence, gradually building a knowledge of the interdependencies of all things in the world and the role that humans have played in the past and ought to play in the future as custodians of this amazing planet. Their study becomes more reasoned, more imaginative and problem-solving and more active, evolving into a philosophical question that guides their work and study into the twelve to eighteen age group. A philosophical inquiry begins around the questions: who am I, what is my task in this world, what do I need to know, what can I do to make a difference and how can 'we' as a society ensure the well-being of others and our planet? In this way, the thread of Earth stewardship is inextricably linked to the actions and knowledge explored from the very beginning.

Help from the Periphery

The periphery is that part of the child that comes into contact with external reality. The child takes in impressions through the senses and through movement. Help from the periphery means presenting objects and activities is such a way as to evoke purposeful movement on the part of the child, 'We never give to the eye more than we give to the hand.'[05]

Human Tendencies

A central tenet of Montessori philosophy is that human beings exhibit certain predispositions that are universal, spanning age, cultural and racial barriers. These have existed since before the dawn of the species and are probably evolutionary in origin. 'Montessori stresses the need to serve those special traits that have proved to be tendencies of Man throughout history.'[06]

Independence

Not depending on another, 'with various shades of meaning'.[07] Developmental milestones such as weaning, walking, talking, etc. can be seen as a series of events which enable the child to achieve increased individuation, autonomy and self-regulation. Throughout the Four Planes of Development, the child and young adult continuously seek to become more independent. It is as if the child says: 'help me to help myself.'

Indirect Preparation

The way nature has of preparing the intelligence. In every action, there is a conscious interest. Through this interest, the mind is being prepared for something in the future. For example, a young child will enjoy the putting together of various triangular shapes, totally unaware that because of this work their mind will later be more accepting of geometry. Also called remote presentation, the deeper educational purpose of many Montessori activities is remote in time.

Indirect Presentation

It is understood that children learn by watching other children work or by overseeing a lesson given to another. In the same way, they quickly absorb the behaviour patterns and the language used by the family and the neighbourhood children.

Maximum Effort

Children seem to enjoy difficult work, work which tests their abilities and provides a sense of their growing power. They exult in giving their maximum effort. For example, a tiny child will endeavour to carry a tray with a challenging array of glasses or push a heavy wheelbarrow and older children, if allowed to make up their own problems, will choose a challenging equation $(1+2+3+4 ...+10)^2$ rather than a straightforward addition.

Mixed Ages

One of the hallmarks of the Montessori method is that children of mixed ages work together in the same class. Age groupings are based on developmental planes.

Infants are in the Nido and toddlers are in the Infant Community; children from three to six years of age are together in the Children's House; six- to nine-year-olds share the lower elementary and the upper elementary is made up of nine- to twelve-year-olds. Because the work is individual, children progress at their own pace; there is cooperation rather than competition between the ages. It should also be possible for children of all ages to interact with other age groups.

Practical Life Skills and Activities

One of the four areas of activities of the Montessori prepared environment. The exercises of Practical Life resemble the simple work of life in the home: sweeping, cooking, washing, gardening etc. These purposeful activities help the children adapt to their new community, develop a sense of responsibility, learn self-control and begin to see themselves as a contributing party of the social unit. As intellect grows and they work with their hands, the personality becomes integrated as body and mind function as a unit.

Prepared Environment

The Montessori classroom is an environment prepared by the adult for children. It contains all the essentials for optimal development but nothing superfluous. Attributes of a prepared environment include order and reality, beauty and simplicity. Everything is related to the children's or young adults' sizes to enhance their independent functioning. A trained adult and a large enough group of children of mixed ages make up a vital part of the prepared environment.

Presentation

The adult in a Montessori environment does not teach in the traditional sense. Rather, they show the child or children how to use the various objects and then leave them free to explore and experiment. This act of showing is called a presentation. To be effective, it must be done precisely, step by step, and with a judicious use of words. From elementary onwards, children still interact with objects but increasingly explore ideas, classifications and frameworks of intellectual knowledge within which their individual or group explorations can take flight.

Sensorial Materials

The sensorial materials were created to help young children in the process of creating and organising their intelligence. Each scientifically designed material isolates a quality found in the world such as colour, size, shape etc. and this isolation focuses the attention

08
Osterkorn. 1980

09
Hellbrügge. 1979

10
Groos. 1901

on this one aspect. The child, through repeated manipulation of these objects, comes to form clear ideas or abstractions. What could not be explained by words, the child learns by experience working with the sensorial materials.

Simple to Complex
A principle used in the sequence of presentations in a Montessori classroom. Children are first introduced to a concept or idea in its simplest form. As they progress and become capable of making more complex connections, they are eventually able to handle information that is less isolated.

Socialisation
'The process by which the individual acquires the knowledge and dispositions that enable him to participate as an effective member of a social group and a given social order.'[08/09]

Work
From an evolutionary perspective, the long period of childhood exists so children can learn and experiment in a relatively pressure-free environment. Most social scientists refer to this pressure-free experimentation as play,[10] although Montessori preferred to call this activity the work of childhood. Children certainly are serious when engaged in the kind of play that meets developmental needs and, given freedom and time, will choose purposeful activities over frivolous make-believe ones.

Work Cycle (minimum three hours)
Through years of observation around the world, Montessori came to understand that children, when left in freedom, displayed a distinct work cycle which was so predictable it could even be graphed. This cycle, with two peaks and one valley, lasted approximately three hours. In Montessori schools, children have three hours of open, uninterrupted time to choose independent work, become deeply engaged, and repeat to their own satisfaction.

Using this book

In earlier times, in Ethiopia, I became engaged in helping a small town community to build their own school. The work gave me an insight into everyday issues of bringing a community together for the purposeful enterprise of its own interest. On returning to Switzerland and becoming more deeply involved with the work of the Arthur Waser Foundation, I had the opportunity to extend this insight in a very interesting way.

In Africa, the Arthur Waser Foundation pursues an education strategy and considers Montessori education to be a particularly good way of helping children and young people to exercise their right to their own development process and to realise their full potential. The notion of publishing blueprints for Montessori schools, which could be offered to local partners of the Arthur Waser Foundation, was first conceived in 2015 by Arthur Waser himself. He believed that a set of modular architectural plans might lower the cost for design and planning, guarantee an ideal learning environment for children and enhance the Montessori educational approach.

From my experiences in different parts of the world I understood that the building, operation and maintenance of such projects are community acts with an inter-generational dimension. With regard to sustainability, a sense of ownership within a community is vital and a project should be a collaborative enterprise executed with the common consent of the population and within the capacity of its human, natural and financial resources. The training and organisation of the local labour forces, the lasting utilisation of regionally available building materials and an environmentally friendly operation are integral parts of educational architecture. It became clear to me that the provision of ready-made architectural plans, regardless of the cultural and environmental context, would not be a step in the right direction to creating a sense of ownership and, for most cases, would be too expensive and too restrictive for any given community.

At the same time, the more I learned about Montessori the more I realised that the educational philosophy ought, naturally, to elicit particular architectural qualities for its schools. The natural consequence of this realisation was that a design instrument based on identifying those architectural qualities would be fruitful to assist those engaged in school design and building. It was at this moment that Steve Lawrence and I met for the first time.

Instead of blueprints, we would deliver a handbook with a spectrum of 'patterns', appropriate for and inspiring to those tackling the recurring architectural problems which the design of educational environments poses.

It is the premise of *Montessori Architecture* that distinct architectural patterns can be recognised, documented and therefore defined in examples of good design practices worldwide; and the Montessori pattern language can be translated into any cultural context and applied regardless of the environmental conditions, economic possibilities or, even, educational approach (in other words, there is no obligation to offer Montessori education in a school which is built accordingly). The result of this premise is that the handbook is not only appropriate for Africa, as it was initially intended, but also for the rest of the world.

METHODOLOGY

In order to prove the basic premise of *Montessori Architecture* – i.e., that universal qualities exist across Montessori schools worldwide – it was necessary to survey a variety of schools in different parts of the world. For this reason the Association Montessori Internationale in Amsterdam, the global authority on Montessori education and widely regarded as the custodian and cultivator of the Montessori pedagogy, prepared a list of recognised reference institutions according to the following criteria: (1) It should cover all four Planes of Development (infancy, childhood, adolescence and transition to adulthood) and therefore involve infant schools, in Montessori called Children's Houses, as well as schools; (2) It should include examples from at least three different continents including Africa; (3) It should comprise both bespoke learning institutions and successfully converted facilities; (4) It should consist of buildings designed by both women and men of different ethnicities; and lastly, (5) All the reference institutions should be symbols of pride for the Montessori movement in different ages.

Herman Hertzberger, a former Montessori pupil and famous for his body of school designs and the author of several books on the design of educational spaces, provided further suggestions for the final catalogue of reference institutions. Two schools, one in Burkina Faso and one in Bangladesh, are not formal Montessori institutions but share the same pattern language and were designed with the involvement of Montessori pedagogues.

To conduct field studies, schools on three different continents were surveyed and other relevant architects such as Anna Heringer, Diébédo Kéré and Richard Partridge were interviewed. In all the countries visited for the purpose of this work – the Netherlands, Belgium, the United Kingdom, Burkina Faso, Sri Lanka, Bangladesh and Tanzania – children showed a remarkable consistency of behaviour in their varied environments, and despite a broad spectrum of conditions, the Montessori architects, designers and builders have achieved a comparable quality of space in them. The book, the website, the drawings and the photographs are an attempt to describe the most relevant underlying reasons for these results. None of the reference learning institutions enshrines a complete list of patterns, and nor do we know what a complete list might be, but drawing on the reviews the patterns published are the most common amongst them.

FORMAT

The book is in two parts; the first part contains the *Montessori Patterns* themselves, organised in a hierarchy of seven levels, with a total of twenty-eight distinct architectural patterns which can be directly distilled from the explanatory observations. The sequential order of the patterns has been put together to serve as a reference during the design process. For convenience and clarity, each pattern has the same format. Next to an exemplar plan sketch, which indicates the respective step, there are three explanatory paragraphs, concerning the design procedure, the underpinning idea and examples.

The final part of the book, 'Repertoire', consists of an inventory of schools visited, surveyed and photographed to provide working examples of the *Montessori Patterns* in use. The repertoire includes one project under construction in Tanzania, which is the winning design of a 2019 competition open to all regional architects who agreed to develop design proposals by testing a prototype version of this book and to provide feedback with regard to its relevance and usability. The description for each Children's House or school consists of a survey report following the sequential order of the observed patterns, comparable data and photographs, as well as floor plans and sectional drawings at standardised scale.

Benjamin Stæhli

Patterns

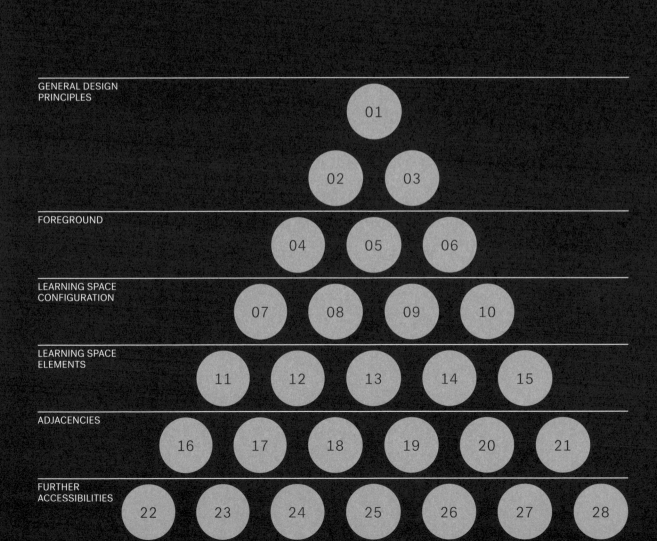

GENERAL DESIGN
PRINCIPLES

01

02   03

FOREGROUND

04   05   06

LEARNING SPACE
CONFIGURATION

07   08   09   10

LEARNING SPACE
ELEMENTS

11   12   13   14   15

ADJACENCIES

16   17   18   19   20   21

FURTHER
ACCESSIBILITIES

22   23   24   25   26   27   28

Montessori Architecture is different from the architecture we associate with conventional educational settings. At the heart of Montessori pedagogy is the idea of the Prepared Environment. Children adapt to their environment and so it follows that the environment must be 'prepared', to be the best it can be, for that adaptation to take place.

The Montessori environment has the purpose of facilitating the natural disposition that all children have to develop themselves. Their natural instincts will take them on an optimal path and the environment must nurture that innate drive and not be an obstacle to it.

The teachers in the Montessori environment take the role of guides for the children and to do this they have to be able to observe all the children easily. The art of teaching in such an environment is to intervene, guide and encourage only when necessary and simply observe and record progress otherwise. Teachers in the Montessori paradigm must also have the self-confidence to allow children to work independently and out of their sight on occasion. This is a mindset diametrically opposite to the conventional rule, sanction and control regime which so often prevails elsewhere. Discipline in the Montessori classroom isn't extrinsic, it's intrinsic, it comes from within the children, it is self-discipline which is derived from confident independence and an innate understanding of natural interdependence.

In a conventional paradigm of extrinsic control, interconnected spaces become counter to functionality because visual and sound isolation are thought to be desirable characteristics, Consequently, a corridor and cellular classroom configuration becomes the default architectural model. A Montessori classroom is not subject to these limitations. In a paradigm where freedom of movement and freedom of choice are pedagogical imperatives, a different kind of architecture naturally emerges. It is an architecture derived from the needs of the child and it follows that it is an environment to which the child adapts most naturally.

This thinking gives us the first of our *Montessori Patterns* which responds to the demands of freedom of movement and freedom of choice, and we call it the Hierarchy of Interconnected Spaces. A knowable domain, resulting from this kind of thinking, will from the child's perspective provide order to which they can orientate themselves, engendering the deep confidence for exploration further afield. It is also the pattern, identified in the preface, which emerged in Maria Montessori's own early communications with architects.

It's obvious that the idea of single age-group classrooms, with a teacher instructing all children at the same time from a blackboard at one end of the room, is a world apart away from our ambition. The idea is not to have the teacher as a focus of attention but rather to have the teachers melting into the background, supporting peer-to-peer collaboration in a multiplicity of work situations on the floor, at a desk, on a window-seat, in an alcove, under a pergola or in the garden.

01
A note, signed by
Maria Montessori, on
Ad Grimmon's drawings
circa 1920 identifies
dimensions of rooms.

This approach leads quite naturally to different architectural forms and the profound effect on the child who is busy with his or her work should not be underestimated. A key to understanding the patterns is to be clear that there is no one-to-one relationship between the patterns and individual spaces, or a schedule of accommodation, but rather that they apply in an inter dependent generality. They may be more or less applicable across the physical environment. They are not prescriptive and not all will necessarily appear, but a majority will tend to. With this background to the idea of the *Montessori Architectural Patterns* in mind, it's interesting to reflect on what Montessori herself had to say:

'The first essential for the child's development is concentration. It lays the whole basis for his character and social behaviour. He must find out how to concentrate, and for this he needs things to concentrate upon. This shows the importance of his surroundings, for no one acting on the child from outside can cause him to concentrate. Only he can organise his psychic life. None of us can do it for him. Indeed, it is just here that the importance of our schools really lies. They are places in which the child can find the kind of work that permits him to do this.

'Any enclosed space, of course, favours concentration. The entire world over, when people wish to concentrate, they seek a place set aside for it. What do we do in a shrine or a temple? These create an atmosphere favourable to concentration. They are forcing houses for character formation. Children are seldom admitted to the ordinary schools before they are five and then the most formative period is over. But our schools offer the tiniest a sheltering refuge in which the first elements of character can take shape, each of which has its own importance.

'When I first pointed out the great value of an environment specially adapted in this way to the needs of little children, this idea aroused great interest in architects, artists, and psychologists, some of whom collaborated with me to settle the ideal size and height of the rooms, and the decorations desirable in a school where concentration was to be favoured.[01] Such a building was more than protective and might almost be called "psychological". Yet its value did not depend entirely on dimensions and colouring – which are not enough in themselves – but it depended on the things provided for the children's use, for the child needs tangible things on which to focus his attention. Yet these things, in their turn, were not decided upon arbitrarily, but only as a result of prolonged experimentation with children themselves.

'We started by equipping the child's environment with a little of everything and left the children to choose those things they preferred. Seeing that they only took certain things and that the others remain unused, we eliminated the latter. All the things now used in our schools are not just the result of elimination in a few local trials but in trials made in schools all over the world. So, we may truly say that these things have been chosen by the children. We found there were objects liked by all children, and these we regard as essential. There were others that they seldom used, contrary to the beliefs of most adults, and this also happened in all countries. Wherever our normalised children were allowed to choose freely, we always obtained the same results, and I used to think of those insects which only, and always, got to the particular flowers that suited them. It was very clear that the children needed these things. A child chooses what helps him to construct himself. At first we had many toys, but the children always ignored them. There were also many devices for displaying colours, but they chose one type only, the flat silk-wound spools we now use everywhere. In every country this was confirmed. Even as to shape and intensity of the coloured area, we let the children's preferences guide us. This close determination of all the objects provided has its reflection also in the social life of the class. For if there are too many things, or more than one complete set for a group of thirty or forty children, this causes confusion. So, we have few things, even if there are many children.

'There is only one specimen of each object, and if a piece is in use when another child wants it, the latter – if he is normalised – will wait for it to be released. Important social qualities derive from this. The child comes to see that he must respect the work of others, not because someone has said he must, but because this is a reality that he meets in his daily experience. There is only one between many children, so there is nothing for it but to wait. And since this happens every hour of the day for years, the idea of respecting others, and waiting one's turn, becomes a habitual part of life, which always grows more mature.'

Maria Montessori — The Absorbent Mind

General design
principles

Pat. 01 A hierarchy of interconnected spaces ... adapted to children's activities

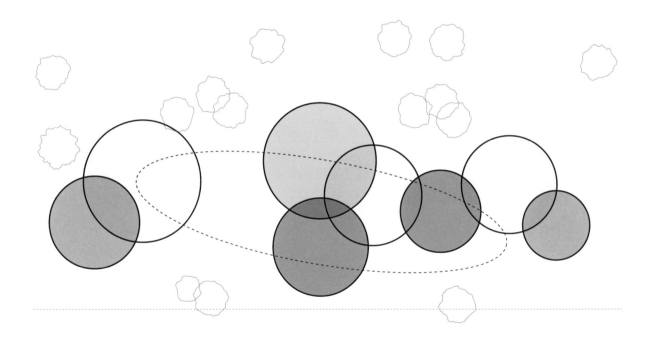

0 1 3 5   10 m   1:400   Example drawing: Haus der Kinder, Vienna

Idea   This is our foundational pattern and it derives from the child's psychological needs. At the core of our approach to *Montessori Architecture* is an attitude of never underestimating the child's sensitivity to his or her environment. In order to feel secure, the child must be surrounded by 'knowable space'. The exploration of the space must be at the child's own volition. The child must be free to move in and around the space so the environment must be adapted to the child's needs, because in turn the child will adapt to the environment. The 'Prepared Environment' is a key concept in Montessori pedagogy and therefore our foundation. At its simplest, our concern is with the environment, the child within the environment and the relationship of the child with the trained Montessori teacher in the environment.

Tasks   To create a 'knowable space' we must have in mind the articulation of that space and the elements which foster a sense of secure orientation within it. We can do this by creating a 'hierarchy of interconnected spaces'. Orientation can be achieved in different ways with directional spaces Pat. 07 or centralised spaces, tall spaces or low spaces, small spaces or big spaces; we are confined only by the parameters of the location and any existing structure. From the child's perspective we are thinking of how the disposition of space creates 'knowability' and our ambition is a 'hierarchy of interconnected spaces' which fulfil the formal use requirements and allow an orientating understanding to develop in the child's mind. It is also our obligation to introduce sufficient complexity to meet the child's curiosity and to design space which meets the child's needs for gross motor activity Pat. 23.

Examples   The *Montessori Architectural Patterns* provide a starting point for the design exercise of creating the hierarchy of interconnected spaces. A front entrance to the east Pat. 04, a greeting space Pat. 05, a garden to the west Pat. 26, differing floor and ceiling levels Pat. 02, daylight and skylight Pat. 16, sufficient floor space for working on the floor Pat. 08. All these individual patterns contribute to achieving a successful hierarchy of interconnected spaces.

Pat. 02 Different heights for floors and ceilings ... even within a single storey

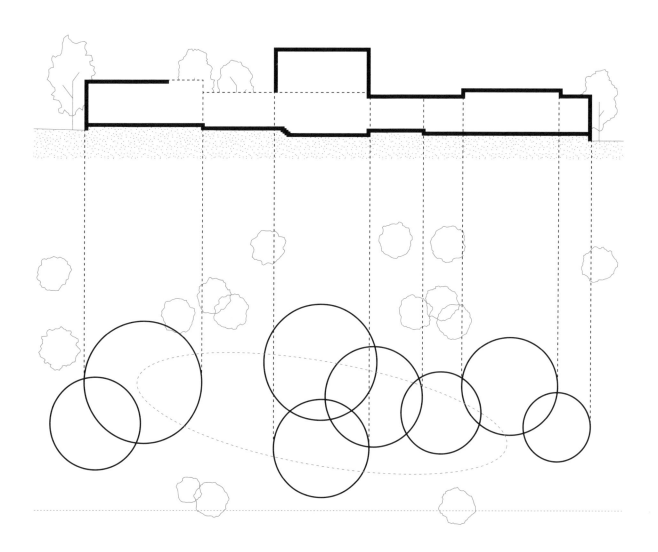

0 1 3 5 10 m 1:400

Example drawing:
Haus der Kinder, Vienna

Idea   From the very beginning in the design process, the Children's House or school should be seen as three-dimensional. In *Montessori Architecture*, interconnected spaces represent a landscape providing topographical experience. Sectional sketches emerge side by side with the floor plan [Pat. 01].

Tasks   Space can be articulated by raising or lowering sections of floor and ceiling; this is true even in single-storey buildings. It is important to give particular thought to the transitions between different levels, designing these wherever possible as tiers of seating with intervening steps in places where stairs are required. Steps, mezzanine levels and balconies can both open up views and provide protection, satisfying the condition for places that not only attract children to them, but also sustain them with a comforting sense of security [Pat. 07].

Examples   In all the schools visited in the preparation for *Montessori Architecture*, steps between different floor heights were occupied by children of all ages and in all circumstances as workplaces and gathering spaces. Ceiling heights were observed to be higher or lower, to compress or expand the spatial impression, creating a sense of intimacy or expansiveness. Wherever sitting-steps were installed to bridge the differences in height of an entire storey or half-storey, as in the Apollo Schools in Amsterdam, there emerged a kind of theatre that encouraged spontaneous activity as well as providing seats for presentations without the need to move chairs around.

Pat. 03   Use of indigenous materials
... with an appreciation
of tactile qualities

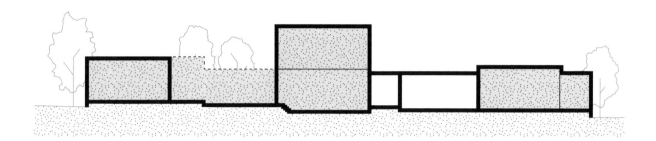

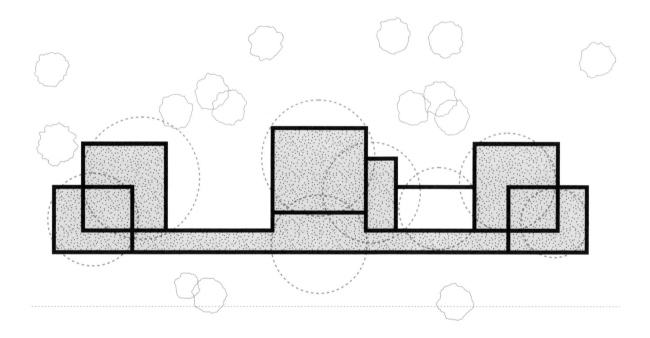

0 1 3 5   10 m   1:400   Example drawing:
Haus der Kinder, Vienna

01
AMI School Standards.
Association Montessori
Internationale-USA
(AMI-USA). Retrieved
22 April 2011

02
Lili E. Peller-Roubiczek,
pedagogical remarks,
'Haus der Kinder',
Vienna

Idea   A critical early decision is often to do with the choice of building materials. It must be an early consideration because the choice of materials and subsequent building elements determines, to a large degree, the range of possibilities in the shape and dimensions of the design [Pats. 01/02].

Tasks   One of the essential elements in Montessori education is learning by doing. In the Montessori environment, children learn concepts and develop their cognitive and motor skills by working with physical materials and artefacts.[01] Absorbing information, as they do, through touch, children are highly attuned to the tactile quality of the building surfaces around them. There is inherent beauty in the roughness, simplicity, modesty and intimacy of natural substances such as wood or stone. The Montessori sensorial learning materials, used in the Montessori classroom, are manufactured from natural materials to help children develop and refine their senses. It is natural that the same thoughtful approach is taken towards building materials used to form the children's environment.

Examples   An appreciation of the integrity of indigenous natural materials is also culturally relevant. The self-reliance of a community is an indisputable demonstration of its coherence and, for the child, invaluable for the development of his or her own self-esteem.[02] In all of the *Montessori Architecture* reference projects we can see the cultural connection created by the buildings because they have been constructed with the human and natural resources of their immediate environment. For example, we see the use of bamboo in Bangladesh, compacted earth in Burkina Faso, stone in Belgium and indigenous timber in southern England. The thick earth walls at the METI School in Rudrapur, as well as at the Gando Primary and Secondary School, satisfy the need for pleasantly cool learning environments in spite of the heat outside the buildings. These thick walls, made from indigenous materials, mean there is no dependence on air-conditioning, reducing operational costs and constituting good earth stewardship.

Foreground

Pat. 04 Orientation of the entrance
...towards the morning sun

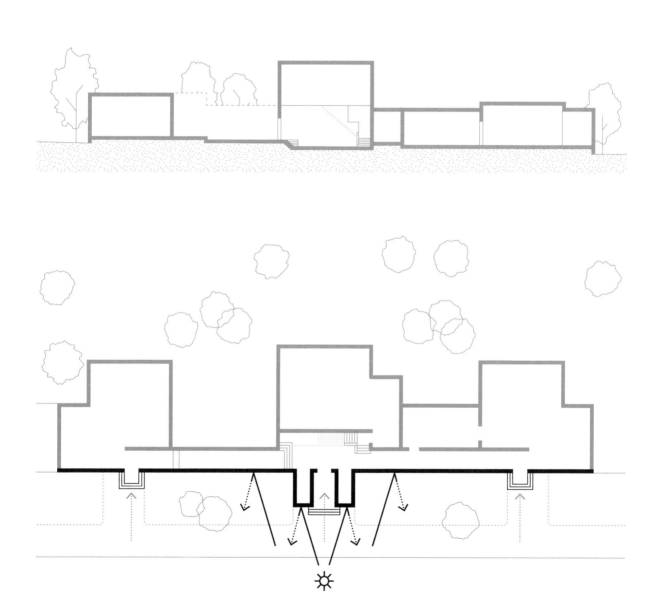

0 1 3 5   10 m   1:400   Example drawing:
Haus der Kinder, Vienna

Regardless of culture, religion, ethnicity or geographical location, for every human being on this planet, the sun rises in the east. The orientation of the entrance so it catches the early rays of the sun each day is an example of the universality of the Montessori architectural approach. A door, passage or gate can be formed in a multitude of fashions and materials; with the right orientation, however, children will approach a school or Children's House lit in sunlight, entering the building with a positive energy.

Tasks At first sight, this may not always be possible because the vicinity only provides access from other directions, for instance. Nonetheless, this problem often presents the opportunity to be creative and to produce something really interesting, such as introducing special angles or shapes for the facades. The building does not necessarily have to be aligned with the site's boundaries, nor does the entrance to the building have to be on the boundary of the property. There can be a path around the building, providing a sort of dramatic experience and making the way to the school even more interesting.

Examples The orientation of the entrances to the morning sun is an evident pattern for all the repertoire projects. In the case of the Apollo Schools in Amsterdam, one of the two buildings is facing north although its outside staircase is turned to the east. (The Apollo Schools were built as twin schools; only one of them is a Montessori school but both exhibit *Montessori Patterns*.) The access to the property of the METI School in Rudrapur is located in the north (to the only road of the village), but, hidden by trees, children walk around the building before arriving in front of the east facade. Some schools, such as the International Montessori School in Tervuren, even have dedicated exits to the west of the buildings, in order to achieve the result of leaving the school bathed in evening sun.

Pat. 05 Connecting function of the greeting space ... to avoid corridors

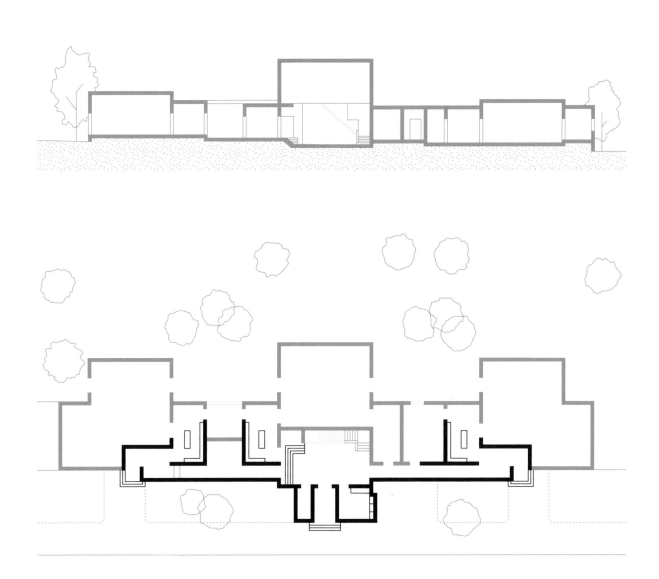

0 1 3 5   10 m   1:400   Example drawing:
Haus der Kinder, Vienna

Idea   Coordinating with the design of the entrance [Pat. 04], the adjacent greeting space can be similarly configured with the child's psychological well-being in mind. A sense of place, encompassing psychological transition from the outside to the inside world, can be created where the adult welcomes the child. It is important to understand that this is not a corridor for just passing through; in *Montessori Architecture*, the greeting space may be compared with the lobby of a hotel – an open intermediate space, which not only connects all the rooms (sometimes even on several floors), but welcomes guests and, in itself, provides a pleasant space to linger.

Tasks   Learning is not confined to the classrooms and there are as many activities outside as inside and in intermediate spaces [Pat. 20], so it is important to design the greeting space in such a way to encourage its use for work [Pat. 13]. Often the greeting space also provides wardrobe facilities and hooks and hangers for each child so they can be independent in changing their clothing and footwear. Achieving this balance between different spatial conditions is the most important task of the architect. If the Children's House consists of only a single room, which may be the case, it is the greeting space.

Examples   Typical of buildings by Herman Hertzberger, the Apollo Schools combine the greeting spaces (Hertzberger refers to them as 'Streets of Learning') with indoor amphitheatres [Pat. 22]. Sometimes, as in the Gando Primary and Secondary School, this space is located outside, protected by an array of air-cooling trees or, in the case of the International Montessori School in Tervuren, we find a courtyard (originally a farmyard) surrounded by all the classrooms (originally barns).

Pat. 06 Avoidance of doors
...but with respect for privacy

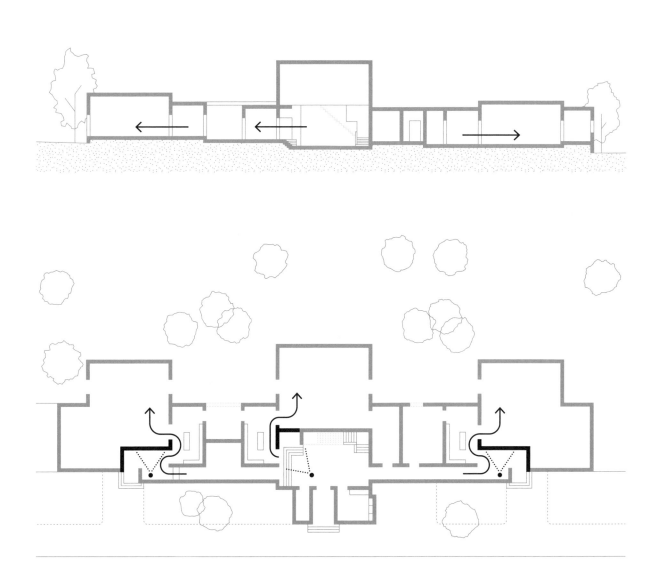

0 1 3 5   10 m   1:400   Example drawing:
                                  Haus der Kinder, Vienna

Idea   In combination with the principle of interconnected spaces [Pat. 01] and the function of the greeting space [Pat. 05], the avoidance of physical barriers such as doors is essential in *Montessori Architecture*. There is always a spatial connection between different areas, while still accommodating divergent territorial uses [Pat. 07].

Tasks   Instead of doors, the architect works with room shapes to create a degree of seclusion and, at the same time, to provide interesting views and relationships. Between different rooms, it is possible to create threshold zones, which achieve spatial articulation rather than closure, and ensure smooth transition between, for example, the greeting space and classroom. With the classroom opening up and the children spreading out, the learning space as a whole becomes bigger. If, to meet official rules and regulations, doors are required, sliding doors can be installed, or small doors within doors, or stable doors, or concealed doors within the walls which can be left open without being noticed. For toilet cabins, or whenever additional privacy is desired, half doors can be provided [Pat. 19].

Examples   Most of the surveyed repertoire projects successfully avoid internal doors. In Gando and Rudrapur, where classrooms have their own access from the outside, doors are kept open during lessons. The same is mostly true for the Apollo Schools and the International Montessori School, where Dutch and Belgian fire regulations, respectively, required some internal doors. In the Montessori College Oost, Herman Hertzberger reluctantly installed doors between the greeting space and the classrooms but included porthole-shaped openings to provide a degree of connection.

63

Learning space
configuration

Pat. 07 Articulation of space and form ... to create islands of concentration

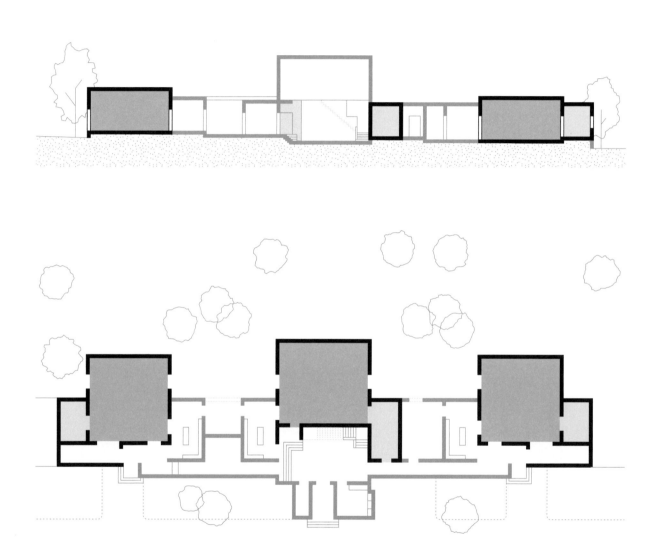

0 1 3 5   10 m   1:400   Example drawing: Haus der Kinder, Vienna

Idea   Creating interconnected spaces, by omitting partitions and barriers between classrooms, may impact the social pattern but it is not enough to produce a satisfying learning environment. While it is essential to give groups and individuals working alongside each other the necessary privacy for focused attention, *Montessori Architecture* puts a distinct emphasis on the articulation of space and form. The aim is to create islands of concentration.

Tasks   Articulation will involve coherent fragmentation into smaller spatial components which are able to take on their own distinguishable properties and qualities – using wall shapes, different floor heights [Pat. 02], built-in shelves, local area lighting [Pats. 17/18] or a change of building materials [Pat. 3]. As this adds to the complexity, the architecture has to secure a visual unity that manages to draw together spatially the parts from which the whole is assembled. The more children work individually, and the more the space they work in is tailored to these conditions by being articulated, the greater the need to retain a clear overview of the whole.

Examples   Many of the visited Montessori schools, such as the St. Bridget's Montessori School in Colombo or the International Montessori School in Tervuren, organise open rectangular plans by creating enclosures separated by low shelves. Anna Heringer and Herman Hertzberger work with different room shapes to provide nooks, niches and alcoves where one or more pupils can concentrate on their own activity. At the other end of the spectrum, the Primary and Secondary School in Gando comprises only small, connected rooms, so they can each be made available to another group.

Pat. 08 Use of the floor as a primary workplace

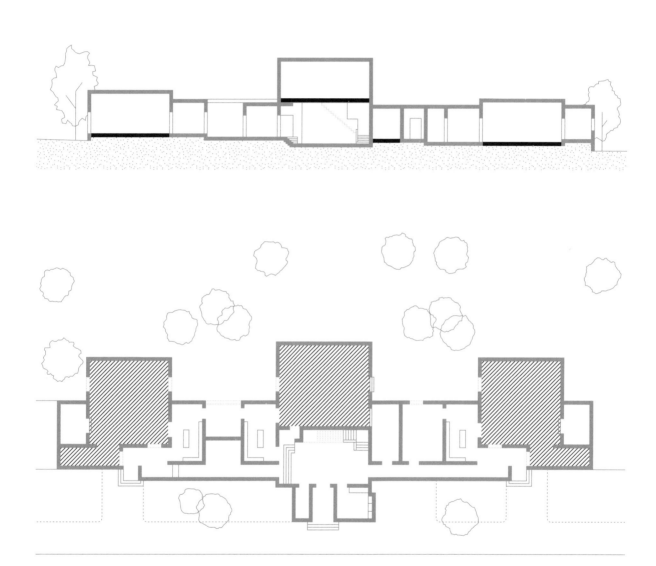

0 1 3 5 10 m 1:400

Example drawing:
Haus der Kinder, Vienna

Pat. 02 ↗p. 52
Different heights for
floors and ceilings…

Pat. 03 ↗p. 54
Use of indigenous
materials…

Pat. 07 ↗p. 66
Articulation of space
and form…

Idea   Visually, the most obvious difference from traditional western education is that Montessori children will use the floor as their primary worktop. They can claim a temporary place of their own for a particular self-chosen activity by rolling out a small piece of carpet or rug onto an open patch of floor. Observation confirms that there are many activities that children naturally prefer doing on the floor. In *Montessori Architecture*, the school design has to provide ample space and the appropriate conditions to work on the floor having regard to the choice of material [Pat. 03], cleanliness and temperature.

Tasks   Steps and sunken spots are particularly helpful to activate the floor as a work area [Pat. 02]. The generally 'lost' space under stairs can also be accessed and used when the floor area is made slightly deeper below the bottom of the staircase. This can create a sheltered nook with an element of intimacy away from the to-ing and fro-ing of other children. In the Apollo Schools in Amsterdam, the place under the stairs is a coveted spot for a child to withdraw for a while to read a book.

Examples   Most remarkable is the METI School in Rudrapur, where children perform all activities on the floor. Apart from chart boards and chairs for the teachers, there is no other furniture. In the METI School, the floor surface is covered with carpets and bamboo mats. All other referenced Montessori Children's Houses and schools follow the idea of the rugs within an articulated place [Pat. 07]. In addition, the European examples may have floor heating installed to enhance comfort during the cold months.

Pat. 09 Accessibility for children
...of different ages

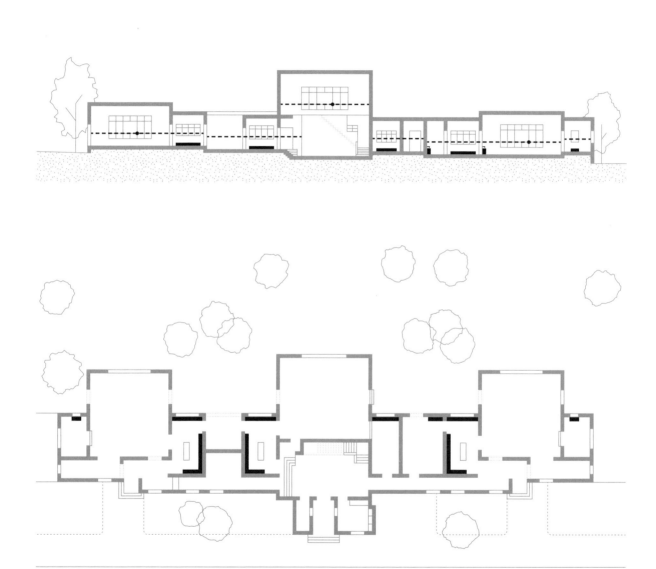

0 1 3 5   10 m   1:400   Example drawing:
Haus der Kinder, Vienna

01
Lili E. Peller-Roubiczek,
pedagogical remarks,
'Haus der Kinder',
Vienna

Idea   As an integral part of their education, Montessori children engage in 'practical life' activities such as basic food preparation, cutting fruit and vegetables, baking, cleaning, washing hands, cleaning the dishes, washing and laundering or gardening. These tasks provide a daily routine and the ideal possibility for children to learn uncomplicated but important tasks for the community. The underlying purpose of these activities is 'to form [the] life and activities of the child in such a way, that motivation – originated from the inner, natural pleasure and profound desire – will be appreciated by the social environment in which [the child] lives'.[01] External spaces such as verandas, patios, tool sheds, raised beds, accessible animal enclosures, safe spaces to study wildlife such as ponds and wild areas should be designed with accessibility in mind.

Tasks   In *Montessori Architecture*, the immediate contact between children and the developmental materials, as well as the independent use of furniture, kitchens and other building elements, have important implications for the design, material, colour and ergonomics of furniture and equipment and, for example, the positioning of building elements such as doorhandles, handrails and windows. There is a distinct difference between 'making everything accessible to children' and 'everything child-sized'. As Herman Hertzberger stresses, children strongly desire to become part of the adult-world. He therefore prefers making adult-sized elements accessible to children. This can be done by introducing a step in front of a window, for instance. A balance needs to be maintained between making things child-sized and making those things that are not child-sized accessible.

Examples   The building designs of all referenced institutions allow the independent manipulation by the children, including the utilisation of toilets, water taps or pumps and kitchens. Whilst the surveyed Montessori Children's Houses follow the principle of 'everything child-sized', with appropriately sized tables and chairs, the design of Montessori schools for young adults over twelve years of age needs to satisfy the urge of adolescents to be recognised as adults.

Pat. 10 Consideration of the acoustical environment ... and the difference between sound and noise

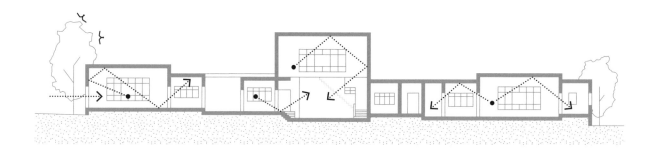

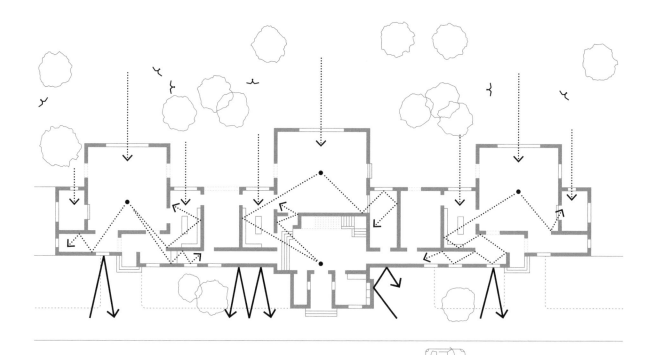

0 1 3   5   10 m   1:400   Example drawing:
Haus der Kinder, Vienna

Idea   The concept of interconnected spaces [Pat. 01] and spatial articulation, rather than providing separated rooms [Pat. 07], requires close attention to the acoustics. In *Montessori Architecture*, the aim is not to generate
a soundless environment but to create a euphonic atmosphere. In sketch-
ing plans, architects consider the flow of sound and the reverberation time
of materials to determine the acoustic quality of a place.

Tasks   In a cathedral, visitors tend to whisper because the shape
and reflective material of the nave cause even the gentlest sounds to echo.
As a consequence, such an environment is usually very quiet, despite the
immensity of the space, allowing people a moment of contemplation and
self-communion. On the other hand, when music is played, the same space
produces a powerful sound. Religious spaces where chanting or singing
are practised also transition from contemplative spaces to reverberating
meaningfully with an intensity of sound. In the same way, architects can
use materials, textures, thickness and shape to create different types of
acoustic environments. Deliberate openings, for instance to the garden,
will allow in the pleasing sounds of bird song or a fountain, while keeping
out the less pleasing noises such as motor traffic.

Examples   The central greeting spaces of the Apollo Schools and the
Montessori College Oost in Amsterdam work in a similar way to the nave
of a cathedral and children tend to be sensitive to and respectful of this.
The thick soil walls of the METI School in Rudrapur can easily absorb the
exuberant voices of the small children, while small openings allow the
chirp and twitter of the birds to enter the rooms for a moment of medita-
tion. The upper floor of St. Bridget's School, Colombo, is beautifully embedded in the soundscape of the neighbourhood, while still establishing
enough quietness for concentration.

Learning space
elements

75

Pat. 11 Use of the walls and building fabric for storage space

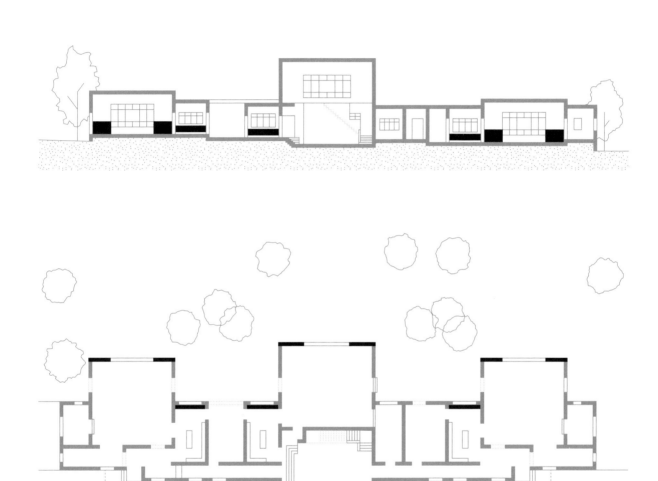

0 1 3   5   10 m   1:400   Example drawing:
Haus der Kinder, Vienna

Idea   Specific to Montessori education is the use of so-called 'sensorially based manipulated materials' which help children to refine their conceptual understanding of the world through the direct experience of movement and their senses. These materials open the way for a weaving of interconnected experiences providing understanding for exploration across many areas of subject matter and can be revisited by children of all ages [Pat. 09]. A child not only works with these materials but has a way to check their own work rather than seeking out the teacher if they have a question as to whether or not they did it right. This is known as self-correction and it promotes independence and problem-solving on the part of the child.

Tasks   At all levels of Montessori education, the children are offered 'concrete' materials that are scaffolded, interconnected and enable exploration of the world and its wonders. *Montessori Architecture* needs to provide sufficient shelving and storage space for all these 'concrete' materials as well as other materials. For example, in a Montessori Children's House environment, children are surrounded by materials such as the Cylinder Blocks, Pink Tower, Brown Stair, Red Rods, Coloured Tablets, Binomial Cube, etc. All of which have a need to be displayed in a particular order and to be accommodated for difference in size. The materials must be clearly displayed across the environment [Pat. 07] and without giving up valuable floor space [Pat. 08]. With this in mind, it makes sense to proportion walls sufficiently deeply to integrate storage and shelf space. In addition, thicker walls tend to have better thermal and acoustic characteristics.

Examples   The Children's House of the Maria Montessori School in London was designed with the exact lengths of all the necessary shelves in mind, with a view to integrating them into the meandering walls. By maximising the storage in this way, the architect was able to create a spacious Children's House on a relatively small footprint area.

Pat. 12 Open storage and display of learning materials

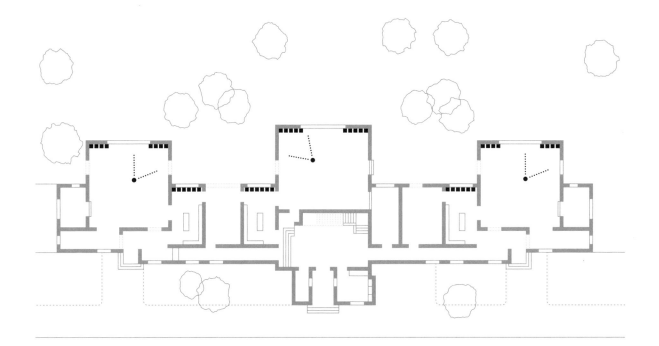

0 1 3 5   10 m   1:400   Example drawing:
Haus der Kinder, Vienna

Pat. 13 ↗ p. 80
Observation without
intrusion

01
Lili E. Peller-Roubiczek,
pedagogical remarks,
'Haus der Kinder',
Vienna

Idea   'Only freely chosen activities are done with a sense of delight and passion.'[01] In Montessori pedagogy, the teacher introduces a variety of areas of learning to the child, who adds them to his or her catalogue of activities. This enables the child to eventually 'choose' activities based on interest. Consequently, the variety of learning materials is as important as their careful selection by the educators. In *Montessori Architecture*, particular attention is paid to the shelving as a room-characterising element, and to the ways in which this shelving, and its organisation for storage, can be an important element in shaping the environment and the way the children use it.

Tasks   Simplicity, lack of clutter and only what is essential are hallmarks of the Montessori aesthetic alongside culturally relevant utensils and artefacts. Any sort of storage should be freely accessible and open even for supplies such as paper, so not only the teacher but also the children are in charge of the stock. Learning materials need to be arranged in an ordered and inviting manner, which allows the child to choose freely and independently without the adult's help. Since the child is urged to put back the material in its right place, an understandable spatial order facilitates this task and enhances the autonomy and self-confidence of the child. Occasionally, low shelves or open cupboards can be used for the articulation of places and to provide screens of privacy [Pat. 13].

Examples   Most of the referenced environments integrate storage space into the walls and use open shelves to create small enclosures inside the rooms. Starting from the perimeter, the St. Bridget Montessori School in Colombo is divided into bays by low, broad, built-in cupboards that are accessible from both sides and can be used to store equipment and crockery. The sensorial materials are kept in these room dividers. The ends of the cupboards are fitted with drawers in which the children can keep their personal belongings.

Pat. 13 Observation without intrusion

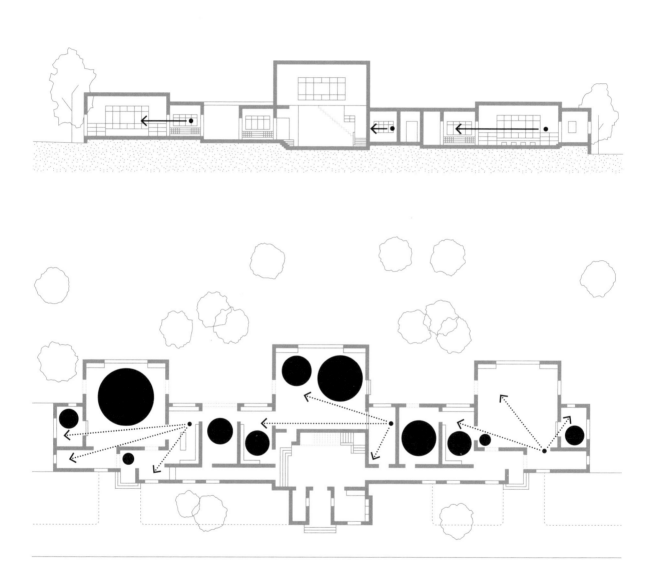

0 1 3   5   10 m   1:400   Example drawing:
Haus der Kinder, Vienna

Pat. 19 ↗ p. 94
Independent self-care ...

01
Müller T. and Schneider R., 2002, *Montessori Teaching Materials, 1913–1935, Furniture and Architecture*

02
A panopticon is a radial layout such as that used in prison design where prisoners can be easily watched by a few guards.

Idea   'Free work' is (...) characteristic of the Montessori school, although teacher led lessons do take place. The children select from a range of possibilities which activity they would like to direct their attention to; they also set their own goals and choose the form of working and the time they would like to spend on it.'[01] In contrast to the traditional education paradigm with its focus on instruction, *Montessori Architecture* embodies the absence of any associations with compulsory learning and restrictions on freedom.

Tasks   The more emphasis shifts from instruction to self-directed learning, the greater the need for the opportunity for children to be able to work either alone, or with others in a group, without an adult's 'interference'. This requires spatial conditions which allow children and young adults to be remote (a polar opposite idea to that of a panopticon).[02] Children must still feel the security provided by the guardianship of the adult and feel connected to their peers. There is a delicate balance to resolve and it can be achieved by spatial devices such as the purposeful addition of building elements to create the feeling of privacy. Interestingly, this not only allows children to feel trusted and independent but also helps teachers to devote more time to any children who might need it.

Examples   The pattern of 'observation without intrusion' is especially important when designing the toilets for the younger children [Pat. 19]. In the Apollo Schools in Amsterdam, for instance, half doors and semi-transparent glass bricks between the toilets and the adjacent classrooms satisfy the children's need for privacy whilst providing the possibility of adult supervision if necessary.

Pat. 14 Offer of seclusion
...and respect of concentrated activity

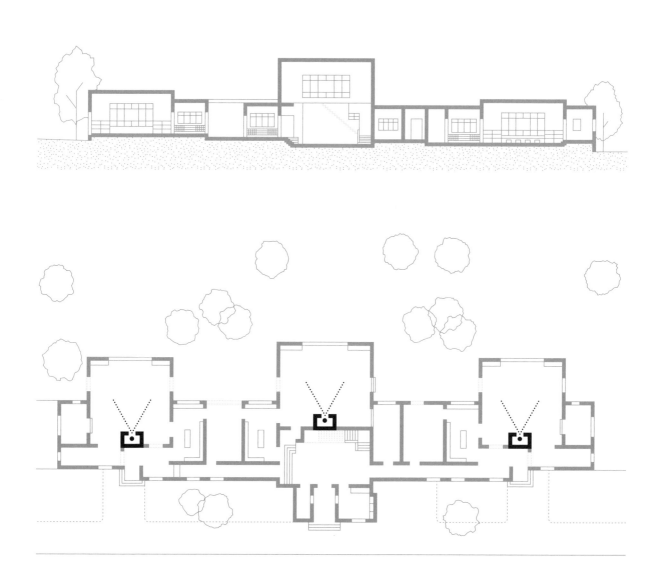

0 1 3   5   10 m   1:400   Example drawing:
Haus der Kinder, Vienna

Idea   The concentration that is needed for a particular kind of learning will depend very much on the type of work. Another important aspect is that the capacity for concentration is also a 'variable'. An environment that is to create the best conditions for learning has to be able to offer various degrees of seclusion for uninterrupted concentration. Children with independence will have the self-confidence to choose appropriate places for the tasks they've selected, and they have a great capacity for working intensely – a child may work on the floor for several hours on a single activity unaware of other activity around, while on another occasion the same child may take a book to a window seat away from other activity.

Tasks   Variety in the spatial provision is highly desirable: niches, alcoves, platforms can provide the psychological space for intense concentration. A degree of boldness is required by the designer, who must have in mind the independence of the child to choose for themselves.

Examples   The Apollo Schools in Amsterdam provide special study places including cosy bunkbed alcoves for reading or napping. In the International Montessori School in Tervuren, children find a special compartment with a door so low that no adult can pass through. The earth walls of the METI School in Rudrapur are deep enough to integrate an organically shaped system of 'caves'. There are also 'secret' places inside the walls of the St. Bridget's Montessori School in Colombo.

Pat. 15 Creation of window seats
...the psychological connection
with the outside world

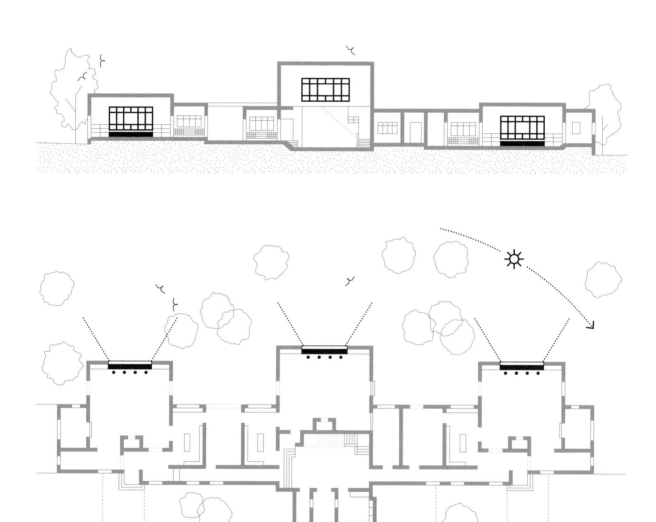

0 1 3 5   10 m   1:400   Example drawing:
                                  Haus der Kinder, Vienna

Pat. 14 ↗p. 82
Offer of seclusion ...

01
Standing, E. M., 1957.
*Maria Montessori:
Her Life and Work.*
New York: Plume

02
Hertzberger, H., 2008.
Space and Learning

Idea   The importance of the relationship between inside and out-side spaces for children in the Children's House was emphasised by Maria Montessori, who described the interaction between classroom and garden or nature outside.[01] This relationship plays an important role in several of the patterns in *Montessori Architecture*; one of them has to do with window seats and windowsills wide enough to become worktops. In this pattern, as in Pattern 14 where we think about niches, nooks and alcoves, and in Pattern 20 where we think about transitional spaces, we have in mind the framing of space to encompass that which is external to it. We bring the outside world into the child's psychological space.

Tasks   Herman Hertzberger identifies the idea of a snail's shell, with its encasing protection inwards and increasing openness outwards, as a theoretical model for the Montessori classroom.[02] If the niche[Pat. 14] repre-sents the most inward-looking kind of place, the window seat is perhaps the most outward-looking. There is a special appeal to working 'almost outside', only protected by a thin layer of glass, membrane or lattice, while still experiencing the comfortable climate of the room. Not surprisingly these workplaces are particularly popular when it rains or snows.

Examples   Dedicated window seats or worktops can be found in all of the surveyed Children's Houses and schools. In the METI school in Rudrapur, pupils can sit on the parapet while gazing through a bamboo lattice. In St. Bridget's Montessori School in Colombo children experience the envi-ronment while working only protected by the roof and a low wall. The Gan-do Secondary School provides special seats on the outside extension of the windowsill. In this way, children can enjoy sitting in the shade of the trees even when the shutter of the window needs to be closed.

Adjacencies

Pat. 16 Importance of daylight
...and its direction

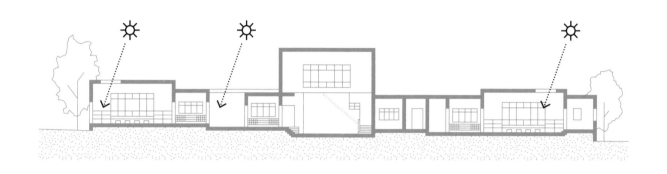

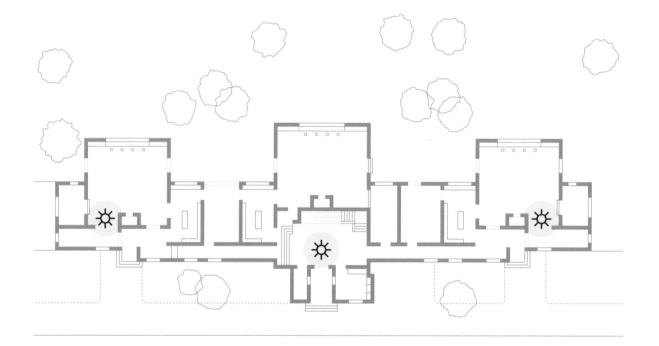

0 1 3   5   10 m   1:400   Example drawing:
Haus der Kinder, Vienna

01
Hertzberger, H., 2008.
Space and Learning

Idea   In *Montessori Architecture*, we find many analogies between, on the one hand, a child's natural and social environment, and on the other hand their prepared educational space. According to Herman Hertzberger, 'once this connection has been made, a train of further associations is released, (...) Corridors become "streets"; interior lighting becomes "streetlighting" and so on.' [01] The 'street' analogy, which frequently arises in Hertzberger's work, reminds us that daylight from above is natural and desirable and we should be sensitive to the possibility of daylight in the rooms from above as well as from the sides where possible.

Tasks   During the day, skylights provide a more natural direction from their source than usual windows built into vertical walls. At an early stage in the design process, daylighting can be considered to bring sunlight to places without it or with limited visual connection to the perimeter, which is especially true for the central greeting space [Pat. 05]. The arrangement and form of skylights may also play an important role in the articulation of places [Pat. 07] and go hand in hand with activity-based lighting [Pat. 17]. Bear in mind that light from multiple directions influences the modelling of objects illuminated and consider how this contributes to the child's understanding of form and shape.

Examples   The new rooms of the Gando Primary and Secondary School have small round openings in the ceiling (which has been cast with traditional jars) and no other windows at all. In this way the walls can keep the immense heat of Burkina Faso outside. In St. Bridget's Montessori School in Colombo, transparent roof sheets are used to highlight places for working in an otherwise dim room. Because of an elongated skylight window, the classrooms in the Apollo Schools in Amsterdam are provided with a constant stream of daylight through the central greeting space.

Pat. 17 Activity-based lighting
...beyond general illumination

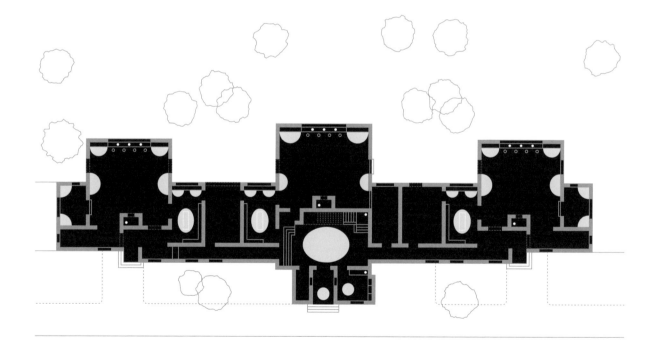

0 1 3 5   10 m   1:400   Example drawing:
Haus der Kinder, Vienna

Idea   In Pattern 7 we looked at the idea of the articulation of places for children's activities. *Montessori Architecture* tends to have a multiplicity of spaces and that, in turn, generates many different conditions requiring activity-based lighting. Reading a book by the window requires a different lighting condition to painting at an easel or lying on the floor engaged in setting out the component parts of a mathematical exercise. Natural light will provide much of what's required, but we can calculate when the component of natural light is insufficient and what supplemental light sources are needed to enhance or substitute the natural conditions.

Tasks   The designer involved with *Montessori Architecture* ought to think beyond 'general illumination' or 'general lighting'; rather, we are concerned with specific activities which may require more detailed consideration. For instance, if an activity involves intense concentration with small pieces of material, that activity will deserve appropriate illumination without detrimental shadows. Maximising natural light is the starting point but a variety of other electrical light sources, some variable in intensity or direction, can supplement and enhance the ambient lighting conditions.

Examples   In secluded corners of the central meeting spaces of the Apollo Schools in Amsterdam there are special work desks with their own activity-based lighting. The same is true for the freestanding sinks which can be found in every classroom. The Children's House of the Maria Montessori School in London mainly works with spotlights to set activity-based light conditions. Both the International Montessori School in Tervuren and the Montessori Place School in Hove, southern England, use little lamps to create small islands and corners for reading.

Pat. 18 Meaningful access to water
...for children

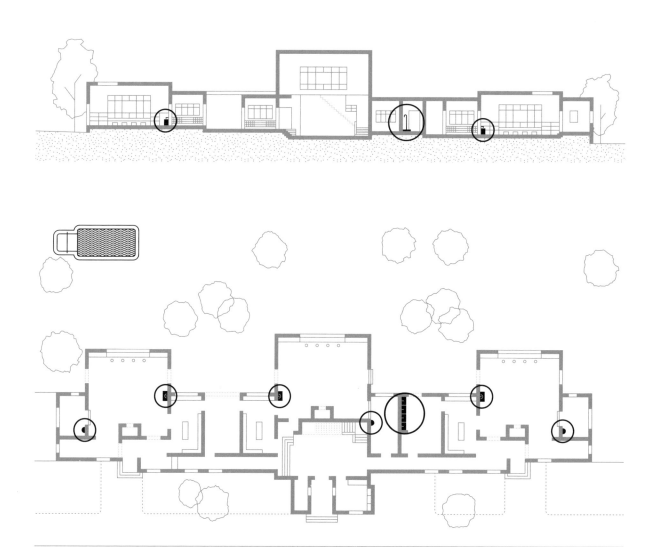

0 1 3   5   10 m   1:400   Example drawing:
Haus der Kinder, Vienna

01
Montessori, M., 1949.
The Absorbent Mind

Idea   Cleaning, washing, cooking, painting, gardening are typical Montessori activities and depend on the use of water. At the same time, all of these exercises also aim to demonstrate the stewardship of resources and the personal responsibilities that are needed for sustainable living. 'Children are inherently attracted to water activities. They love the process of pouring, washing, and transferring water. A child's concentration may be engaged for long periods of time, simply by pouring liquid from one container to another, and back again. (...) It is the child who makes the man, and no man exists who was not made by the child he once was.' [01]

Tasks   As a consequence, *Montessori Architecture* strongly emphasises a free yet meaningful access to potable water both inside and outside classrooms. In wealthier countries this may be taken for granted, but the disposition of water sources should be such that the children have unimpeded access. In schools in arid climates water may be scarce and water collection from roofs or in other ways may be necessary. The natural attention given in Montessori schools to washing hands and general hygiene often means that a cultural attitude is taken home, resulting in a general uplift in community health. Regardless of the scarcity of water, children are encouraged to recycle grey water, so that water is used again for gardening and other purposes. Young adults in Montessori schools are involved in the invention and design of filtration systems, hydroponics and watering systems as part of their interest in Earth stewardship.

Examples   Good examples can be found at the METI School in Rudrapur and the Gando Primary and Secondary School, both locations where drinkable water is a scarce commodity. Here, children have the opportunity to use child-sized hand pumps to pump groundwater to the surface. If a child stops pumping, the flow of water immediately ceases, which clearly demonstrates the direct connection between the personal involvement of the child and his or her access to water. Since it is difficult to pump and make use of water simultaneously, the children in Rudrapur and Gando often work together, experiencing the benefit of collaboration.

Pat. 19 Independent self-care ...understanding of toilets and hygiene practices as part of education

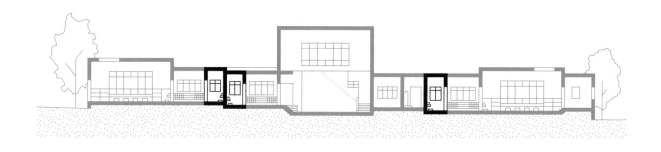

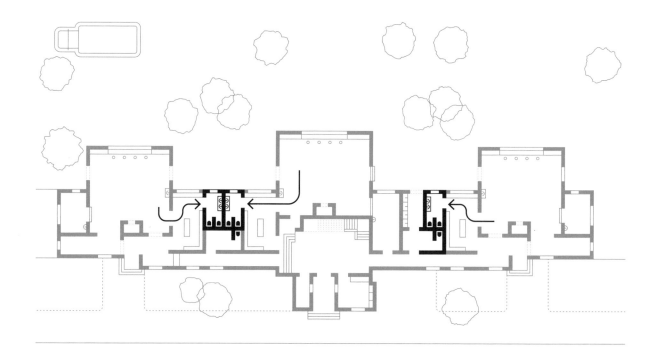

0 1 3 5   10 m   1:400   Example drawing:
Haus der Kinder, Vienna

Pat. 13 ↗p. 80
Observation without
intrusion

01
Lili E. Peller-Roubiczek,
pedagogical remarks,
translated from 'Haus
der Kinder', Vienna

02
Hertzberger, 2017

Idea   Many schoolchildren in developing countries still have no access to proper toilets. Even in Children's Houses and schools in the industrialised world, the provision of toilets is often handled at the level of a basic necessity and usually limited to legally minimum standards with no regard to aesthetics. In *Montessori Architecture*, the use of toilets is understood to be an essential part of education with the capacity for self-toileting an attribute of independence.

Tasks   Toilets used in Montessori environments have to fulfil special requirements. Firstly, they have to provide a certain degree of privacy[Pat. 13] and need to be designed to ensure independent use by children (including helping keep them clean and looking beautiful). Secondly, they should be close by or attached to specific classrooms for children under the age of six. 'For a child, it means a huge difference to be a member of a small community with thirty classmates rather than a tiny member of the masses with hundreds of students (using the toilet for instance). While a sense of responsibility can be acquired for a washbasin which is used by thirty, this is much more difficult for a large cloakroom used by hundreds.'[01] Thirdly, the toilets for children over the age of six have to be placed at the 'right' location, not too far but also not too close to the classroom. 'On the way they see everything that is happening, they see all the different animals and every day they are confronted with it. So, it is not always true that the shortest way is the best. The verdict is, do not spend energy to make it very easy, because what you see is what you know.'[02]

Examples   All visited institutions provide appropriately child-sized toilets (the squat toilets of the Gando and METI schools have smaller toilet pans so children cannot fall into the pits). Many of the Children's Houses and schools use half doors for younger children, which allow them to be unseen whilst using toilets without being completely secluded. In St. Bridget's Montessori School in Colombo, children using the toilets enjoy fresh air and an interesting view of the garden due to the low walls and doors. While the new European referenced Children's Houses tend to make toilets accessible directly from the classrooms, the Gando and the METI schools have toilets in a separate building. The unattended walk from the classrooms to the toilets allows moments of contemplation and helps children to adopt self-sufficiency.

Pat. 20 Transitional spaces between inside and outside ...including shade

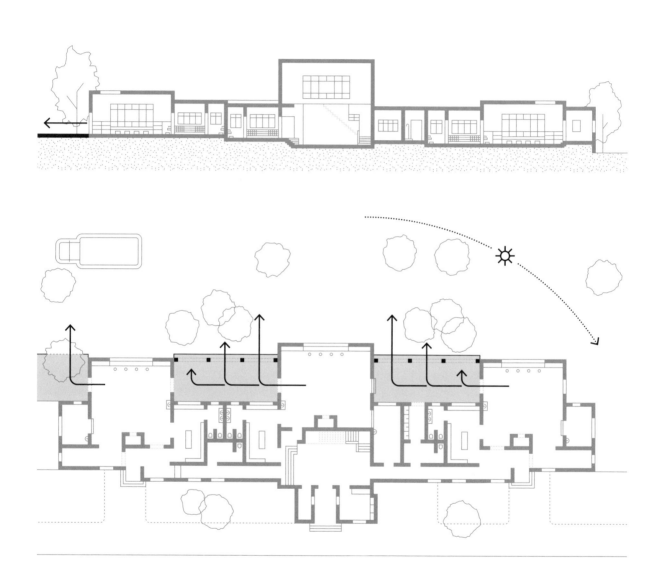

0 1 3 5   10 m   1:400

Example drawing:
Haus der Kinder, Vienna

Pat. 05 ↗p. 60
Connecting function
of the greeting space ...

Pat. 26 ↗p. 110
Earth stewardship ...

01
Hertzberger, H., 2008.
Space and Learning

Idea   If the environment of a school is intentionally designed for projects related to subjects such as biology, ecology, meteorology or geology, children can learn just as much in the open air as inside.[01] In this way, a classroom not only expands into the greeting space [Pat. 5] but also to the garden area [Pat. 26]. In *Montessori Architecture*, much thought is given to the transitional space between the inside and outside of a classroom.

Tasks   Transitional spaces, such as wind-protected and shaded terraces, allow the child to step outside without fully leaving the comfort zone of their classroom. This is also where the interaction happens between classmates and others, since the garden is used by the entire school. These transitional spaces serve as a fresh air extension to the common working areas and are especially suitable for activities involving lots of water which gets spilt and sloshed around.

Examples   In Gando, Rudrapur and Hampstead, London, there are terraces in front of the classrooms. Since the gardens and terraces overlap with the greeting areas, the terraces also serve as transitional zones for the classrooms. In the METI School in Rudrapur, it is the place where pupils take off their slippers, sandals or shoes. In St. Bridget's Montessori School, Colombo, the open upper floor acts as a terrace and, because it is connected by a staircase, it acts as a transitional space between the classroom and the garden.

Pat. 21 Inclusion of a children's kitchen ...and eating tables

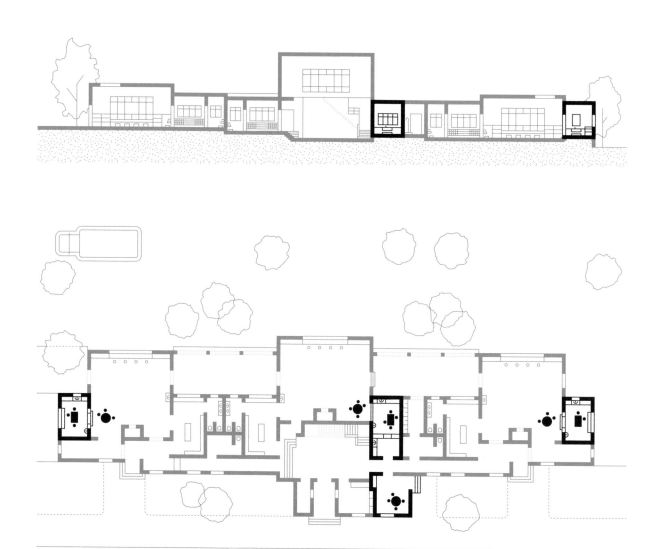

0 1 3 5   10 m   1:400

Example drawing:
Haus der Kinder, Vienna

01
Helming H., 2002,
*Montessori Teaching
Materials, 1913–
1935, Furniture and
Architecture*

Idea   Other Montessori activities that require particular attention in the design process are the 'preparation and serving of meals', 'eating', and 'doing the washing up'. *Montessori Architecture* has to provide places for the preparation of food by children and eating tables for spontaneous use.

Tasks   'The special attention necessary to handle small fragile objects without breaking them, and to move heavy articles without making noise, has endowed the movements of the whole body with a lightness and grace which is characteristic of our children. It is a deep feeling of responsibility which has brought them to such a pitch of perfection. For instance, when they carry three or four tumblers at a time or a tureen of hot soup, they know that they are responsible not only for the objects, but also for the success of the meal which at the moment they are directing.'[01]

Examples   Except for St. Bridget's School in Colombo, children's kitchens can be found in all visited Montessori Children's Houses or schools. In most cases kitchen cabinets have been pushed against walls or into niches to be out of the way and take up as little space as possible. In the Apollo Schools in Amsterdam, however, the placement of small kitchen cabinets in each classroom was used for the articulation of the space. As objects in space, they represent islands which can be approached from all sides. The Apollo Schools show that, when placed freestanding, built-in objects have a structuring effect without dividing the room into detached units (the way walls do).

Further accessibilities

Pat. 22 Everyday gathering spaces
...inside and outside

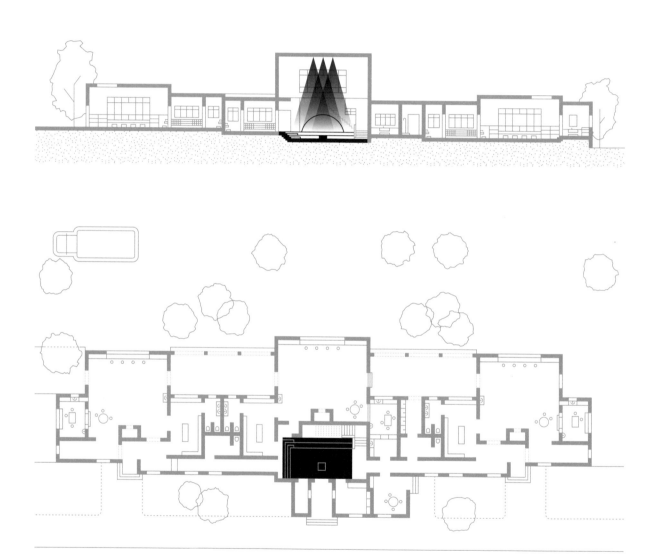

0 1 3 5   10 m   1:400

Example drawing:
Haus der Kinder, Vienna

Pat.01 ↗p.50
A hierarchy of
interconnected
spaces...

Idea   Ceremonial spaces such as assembly halls or theatres are the locations where traditional 'high points' of school life take place. Since it caters only for special events, musical and dramatic performances and so on, an official assembly hall is usually not part of a school's everyday life. Although every school in theory deserves such a facility, it is questionable whether making what is for the most part a sealed-off space is really justified given the reality of the limited means available in education.

Tasks   In *Montessori Architecture*, the challenge is to find a form for a space where performances and productions, ceremonies and celebrations can be integrated with the variety of spaces used for other things. A form is required that creates sufficient accommodation for a demanding activity in what is a comparatively open situation. We can address this by thinking about how to create a space to enhance the 'everyday theatre of life', something which is useful for formal events, but adapted to spontaneous, impromptu, everyday situations such as chatting together, hanging out, using mobile devices, eating and drinking.

Examples   The best examples can be found in the Apollo Schools and the Montessori College Oost in Amsterdam. With his theatre-like organisational design, Herman Hertzberger has created places where children can assemble for official or spontaneous gatherings, large enough to accommodate the entire school if necessary. The shape and form of the theatre invites the children to use it actively as a workplace, a stage for acting, or just a hang-out area. The dense building materials, the wooden surfaces and the complex shapes and volumes of the spaces prevent echoes and enable a pleasing acoustic atmosphere despite the spatial interconnectedness [Pat. 01]. Children at the Gando Primary and Secondary School enjoy a small roof-protected amphitheatre sunken into the stone terrace. The METI Primary School in Rudrapur and the International Montessori School in Tervuren offer small arenas where children can come together. Theatre stages also can be found in Colombo and in Hampstead, London, where steps up to a classroom also form a stage.

Pat. 23 Integration of spaces
for gross motor development
...outside and inside

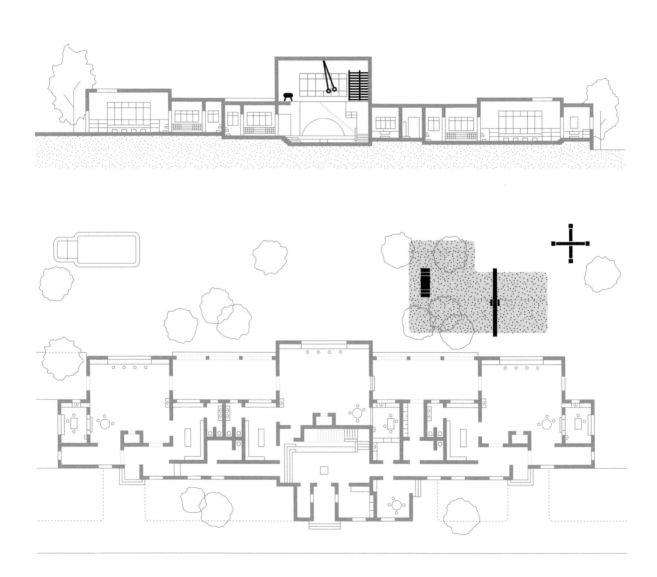

0 1 3 5   10 m   1:400   Example drawing:
                                    Haus der Kinder, Vienna

Pat. 08 ↗p. 68
Use of the floor as
a primary workplace

01
Hertzberger, H., 2008.
Space and Learning

Idea   All the experiences offered in a Montessori environment assume that movement is an integral aspect of learning. Children are born to move. With an emphasis on practical activity, children spend little time sitting on chairs or receiving large group instruction [Pat. 08], so those in a Montessori environment are naturally very active. However, there does need to be a time and place for physical activities such as dance, games or sports. Therefore, the provision of adequate spaces inside and outside the building is as essential as in traditional school systems. *Montessori Architecture* needs to encompass the organic design integration of these spaces.

Tasks   Because of their size, playing fields, gymnasiums or sports halls are usually situated away from school buildings in traditional educational settings. In addition, the rules and regulations concerning the wearing of special footwear or the use of the changing and washing rooms leads to separation of the P.E. spaces from the school, both physically and psychologically. *Montessori Architecture*, on the other hand, should plan for sports facilities to be visually linked to the school, integrated, not separate, but capable of impromptu use at the will of the child. Herman Hertzberger expresses it in this way: 'To effectively integrate sport activities spatially is certain to have a positive effect on the air of activities at school.' [01]

Examples   The Gando Primary and Secondary School, the METI School in Rudrapur and the International Montessori School in Tervuren all provide sports grounds which can be seen from the classrooms. At those schools, children that are watching athletic exercises and games seem to be more inspired and motivated. A similar observation holds true for the schools with a theatre-like space, where having an audience encourages better performances from players and musicians. The Montessori schools in Amsterdam Oost, Pijnacker and Delft also contain indoor gymnasia, which allow physical exercise throughout the year.

Pat. 24 Walking on the Line space
...in the Children's House

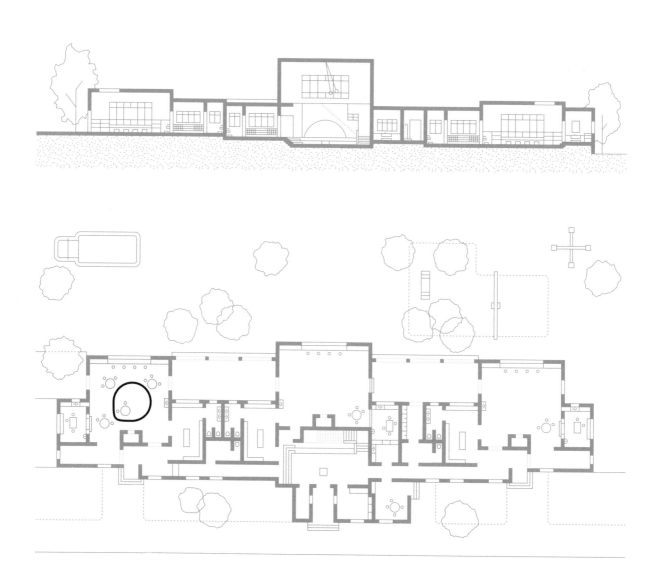

0 1 3   5   10 m   1:400   Example drawing:
Haus der Kinder, Vienna

Pat. 12 ↗p. 78
Open storage and
display of learning
materials

Pat. 23 ↗p. 104
Integration of spaces
for gross motor
development…

01
Helming H., 2002,
*Montessori Teaching
Materials, 1913–
1935, Furniture and
Architecture*

Idea   In line with physical education [Pat. 23] and practical life activities whose purpose is to assist young children in the coordination of movements, mastery of the body and order, Montessori offers an exercise that includes rhythmic movements to music: Walking on the Line. 'The first rhythmic exercises are balance exercises. The children walk like little tightrope walkers along a line that has been drawn in chalk on the floor, usually in the shape of an ellipse. (…) The children are carrying glasses filled with a coloured liquid and the idea of the exercise is to make sure that not a drop is spilled. Sometimes they also carry little bells, which they have to hold so carefully, keeping them still so that they make no sound as they walk. (…) At the beginning, they don't listen to the music at all, or at least they don't relate their movements to it. Gradually they hear and understand the music and their walking and hip movements become more and more related to the music until, without any intervention by the teacher, the movements develop into free dance.' [01]

Tasks   Even though the Walking on the Line exercise may last for as little as ten to fifteen minutes for those children that wish to participate (others may continue working or just sit and watch), the exercise is a permanent offering and a fixed part of the environment. The line is never obstructed and is always available to the child wishing to practise on his or her own, outside the structured group session. In *Montessori Architecture*, the design has to provide the spatial and acoustic conditions (background music may be used) for Walking on the Line spaces inside and outside the building.

Examples   Walking on the Line spaces can be found in all the surveyed Children's Houses. Together with the display of the sensorial material [Pat. 12,] this is one of the visually best recognisable features in *Montessori Architecture* worldwide. Regardless of the country, such a Walking on the Line space contains a smooth elongated elliptical line, which is long enough for ten to twelve children. Inside the main ellipse there may be a concentric ellipse to increase its capacity. The challenge which Walking on the Line presents to very young children should not be underestimated; it involves utmost concentration, poise and self-control.

Pat. 25 School and grounds as a habitat for animals and plants

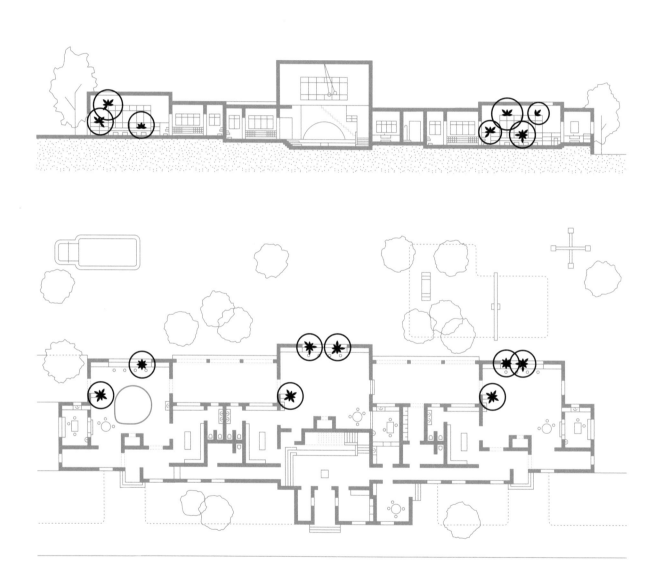

0 1 3 5   10 m   1:400   Example drawing:
Haus der Kinder, Vienna

01
Helming H., 2002,
*Montessori Teaching
Materials, 1913–
1935, Furniture and
Architecture*

Idea   Nature plays an important part in Montessori education. While Patterns 15 and 20 deal with the relationship between the inside and the outside environments, *Montessori Architecture* also actively brings the natural world to the interior and the immediate vicinity of the children. Intramural integration of plants and animals may be of special significance within an urban setting – town or city. 'What is decisive is that freedom granted to the child and the atmosphere of the environment allow him simply to see, absorb, be receptive. This is the basic attitude to nature of the true scholar. The ethos of allowing reality to take precedence over one's own opinion, of not rushing to be of use, but of being receptive to the truth and seeing beauty, should influence.'[01]

Tasks   Another aspect of teaching children about the natural growth and life cycles of many different species which they can observe on a daily basis is the development of responsibility, compassion, empathy and understanding for other life forms. Taking care of plants or animals teaches children to value life other than their own. A further benefit is stress reduction that occurs as a natural response to observing and petting animals, from which both the children and the animals can benefit. Ideally, adequate places and habitats for plants and animals are part of each classroom.

Examples   St. Bridget's Montessori School in Colombo functions as a bird observatory. The entirely open upper floor has the same height as the surrounding trees and invites birds to nest and to use it as a wildlife reserve. In addition, there is an aviary where threatened species of birds are kept. Animals such as cats, dogs, rabbits, chickens, hamsters, gerbils, guinea pigs and a variety of reptiles and fish are found in all of the visited Montessori schools. In the International Montessori School in Tervuren there are ponies which are cared for by the children and in the Apollo Schools in Amsterdam small flowerpots can be found on every desk – each is the responsibility of one of the children. The Montessori Place in Hove, southern England, includes a substantial walled garden with a 'poly-tunnel' where plants are grown for food and for experimentation. Elsewhere in the grounds, at a safe distance, beehives produce honey, and the school has a functioning economic enterprise based around its produce.

Pat. 26 Earth stewardship
...a horizontal pattern

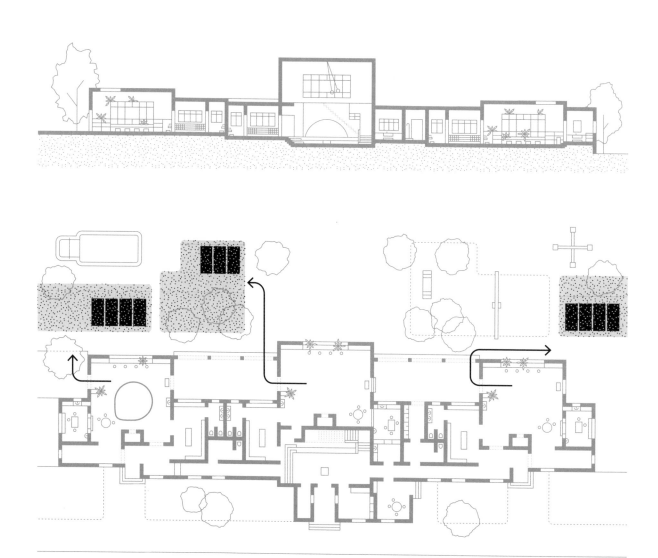

0 1 3   5   10 m   1:400   Example drawing:
Haus der Kinder, Vienna

Pat. 20 ↗p. 96
Transitional spaces
between inside and
outside...

01
Schwarz-Hier E. 1923

02
Wolff J. 2016

Idea   Although gardening is an excellent vehicle to explain the experience of Earth stewardship, the children are engaged from the beginning in multiple experiences, both practical and intellectual, that create in them a love of their environment and a sense of responsibility towards it. In practical terms they are engaged in recycling, gardening and many other forms of environmental conservation for which they are responsible. They explore the interdependencies of all life forms and begin to understand the role that humans play in preserving the health of the planet. A typical Montessori activity is gardening – planting, watering, caring for flowers, vegetables, and so on; the possibilities are endless but depend, of course, on the school's particular environment. What very often is largely an inaccessible 'visual greenery', in *Montessori Architecture* is a purposefully conditioned and cultivated garden for children. 'In Lankwitz the children had a wonderful little garden with lawns to run about on, shady trees, secluded spots, a number of children's flower and vegetable beds, a sand pit and low garden benches. Here they could play freely, observe nature, tend their beds, in summer they were allowed to run around in the sun with no clothes on and in the winter to clear the snow with their own little snow shovels. The beds were there for the children to cultivate however they liked.'[01]

Tasks   Whilst children and young adults can choose to garden at any time, human metabolism tends to slow us down after lunch. Since daylight decreases the production of the sleep hormone melatonin,[02] it makes sense to organise outside activities such as gardening in the afternoon. In view of this, the best approach is to locate gardens to the southwest or west of the buildings, where the children can benefit from the afternoon sun until sunset. In equatorial conditions and where the sun may be too hot, shading devices and wide verandas can be used. This natural orientation of the garden to the west side will also influence the location of transitional inside/outside spaces [Pat. 20]. This aspect of garden orientation may be less easy to realise in a dense urban environment with limited space and overshadowing. In those cases, garden facilities on roof terraces, window boxes or internal gardens may be the only real options.

Examples   A roof terrace garden can be found on top of the Montessori College Oost in Amsterdam. Dedicated west-side gardens for children are part of most surveyed schools or Children's Houses. In the METI school in Rudrapur and the Montessori Place in Hove, children produce vegetables and fruits and even sell part of the harvests to the local markets to enable them to experience the cycle of production and exchange, managing and contributing to their schools. The same is planned for the Gando Primary and Secondary School, where the success will, however, depend on the implementation of a functioning rainwater harvesting, storing and irrigation system.

111

Pat. 27 Children's workshop
...and the materials workshop

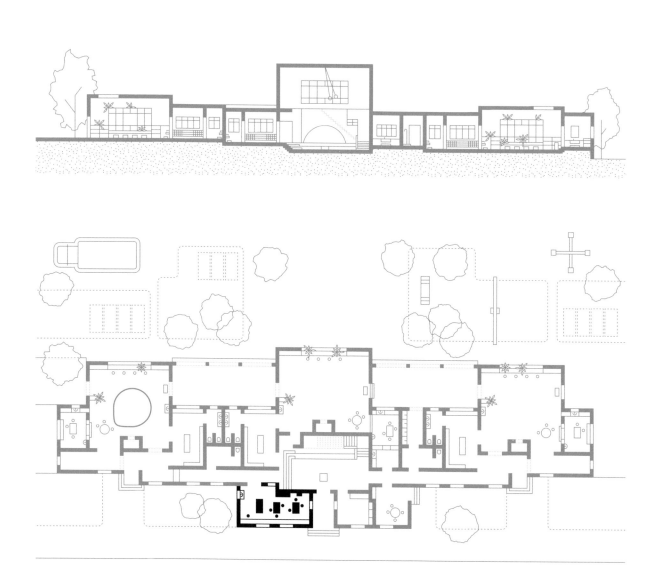

0 1 3   5   10 m   1:400

Example drawing:
Haus der Kinder, Vienna

Pat. 25 ↗ p. 108
School and grounds
as a habitat for animals
and plants

Idea   The need for a workshop in Montessori pedagogy is closely connected to the nature of the materials and their use. Montessori materials are fundamentally different from conventional consumable educational materials and they are used very differently. No material is duplicated; there is only one of each material or piece of apparatus available for the children. The range is vast with well over a thousand pieces of apparatus. Very little is 'consumed' and disposed of, as developmental materials are chosen, used and returned to their place, in the condition they were found, by the children. Montessori children are users of shared materials not consumers of things. From the beginning, children experience the value of natural materials and their limited availability, developing a relationship with the Earth's resources and the necessity to steward them wisely.

Tasks   Workshop(s) therefore have three distinct functions. The first is for the teachers and staff to make the material in accordance with blueprints developed by Maria and Mario Montessori, knowledge of which forms part of every Montessori teacher's training. The second function is for the repair and refurbishment of material that, through frequent use, experiences a high level of wear and tear. The workshop in a developed economy Montessori school, where factory-produced materials are primarily in use, may involve no more than some space given over to minor repairs and repainting. In a developing economy Montessori school, however, the only materials available may be those made in the workshop. In such circumstances the workshop may also extend to being the source of furniture and even building components. It should be understood that the workshop is a source of autonomy for the Montessori school. A third function of the workshop is to be a learning space available for children to help them pursue work they have elected to do; an example may be creating something to help in the care of plants or animals [Pat. 25] or a model of something as part of an exploration of a mechanical apparatus, for example. Children in Montessori education use real things, real crockery, real equipment, and the same is the case in the workshop where real tools are used. This function obviously requires common-sense health and safety attitudes, and tools must be age-appropriate.

Examples   The Pijnacker school near Rotterdam has an external open-sided but roofed workshop where young children can manufacture things using real tools. In the urban Montessori Lyceum at Oostpoort in Amsterdam, workshops for young adults consist of fully equipped wood-working and metal-working workshops. The Oostpoort school, which offers vocational training, incorporates motor transport, healthcare, dance, sound and music workshops. At another Montessori school, the Corner of Hope School in an Internally Displaced People's camp in Nakuru, Kenya, the workshop is staffed by the teachers and a carpenter, and is the sole source of the entirety of the stock of materials and furniture for 250 children.

Pat. 28 Flexibility in furniture layout

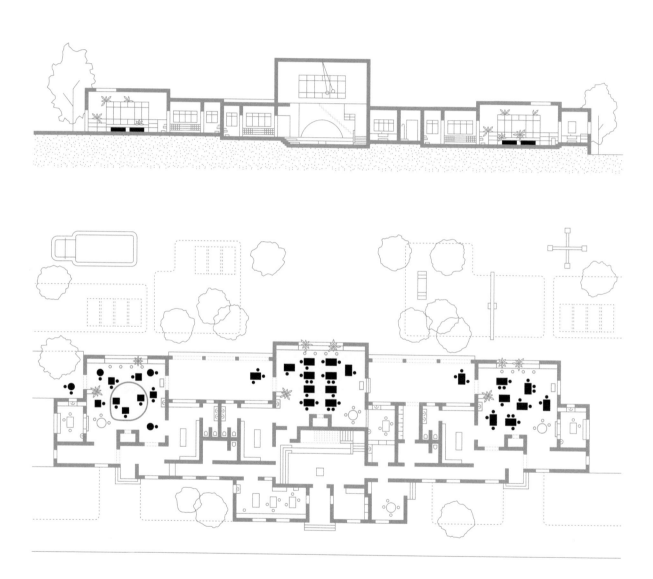

0 1 3 5   10 m   1:400   Example drawing:
Haus der Kinder, Vienna

Idea   The Montessori paradigm is characterised by the independence of children choosing to work where they want to. This can only be possible if the furniture and learning materials can be arranged to suit the independent mind of the child. The architecture will naturally impose restrictions, but if the foregoing patterns have been observed, the resulting architecture will very naturally create significant opportunities for the children to adapt their environment to their own individual and collaborative wishes. Consequently, there is no set layout and furniture is designed to be moved by the children themselves. Occasionally, desks may need to be moved together because a collaborative project is being planned; maybe the work will be individual and intense, involving extensive material requiring extra space, in which case the work may be laid out on the floor and remain there for several sessions of concentrated effort.

Tasks   The environment must be spacious enough to allow this exchange and constant reinvention of layout. The furniture elements must be of a suitable size for children to move independently of adult help. The possibility of stacking is also desirable, with storage space available, so that floor areas can be cleared to create everyday gathering spaces [Pat. 22], gymnastic areas [Pat. 23] or to allow for Walking on the Line [Pat. 24].

Examples   The International Montessori School in Tervuren uses flexible furniture in its converted barn space to great effect as an adolescent workspace for individual work and collaborative work. Curtains across one end conceal staging for music and drama, and sofas and armchairs provide adolescent-friendly workplaces and props for theatre production. A similar approach to the large communal entrance space at Montessori College Oost, with ceiling-mounted curtain tracks, allows the division of space and the introduction of seating for presentations, meetings, concerts and shows.

Repertoire

9 References

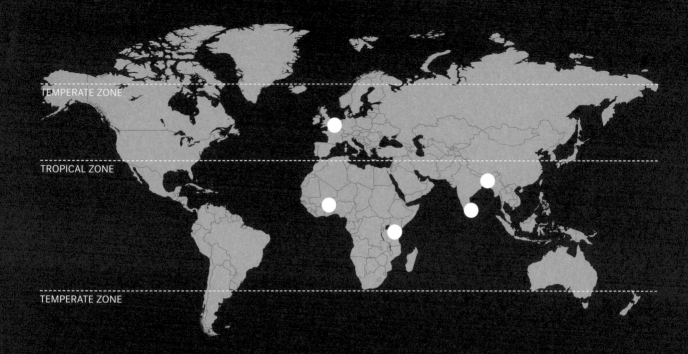

TEMPERATE ZONE

TROPICAL ZONE

TEMPERATE ZONE

TEMPERATE ZONE (DETAIL)

TROPICAL ZONE (DETAIL)

In establishing a repertoire to illustrate the *Montessori Architectural Patterns*, the aim was to draw upon examples from a spectrum of settings, including tropical, subtropical and temperate zones.

Two projects chose themselves, being world-renowned examples, well documented in architectural literature. These were Herman Herzberger's Apollo Schools in Amsterdam and Geoffrey Bawa's school in Colombo.

The Gando, Burkina Faso, and Rudrapur, Bangladesh, projects are by two emerging architects who have been inspired by Montessori principles and have received significant acclaim for their approach.

The projects at Pijnacker in Rotterdam, Hof Kleinberg in Brussels, Hampstead in London and Eason's Green, East Sussex have all been created within existing buildings, which is the most common situation for the creation of Montessori schools so far. Eason's Green and Hof Kleinberg both include adolescent age groups, which are less common. The Hampstead project is part conversion and part extension to an existing building and the Pijnacker project is the reworking of a conventional school.

The fourth project is the as yet unbuilt design for a Montessori campus at Ngabobo, Tanzania, which is the result of an architectural competition based upon a prototype version of *Montessori Architecture*. The competing architects, all from the local community, were asked to explicitly consider, in their design endeavours, the patterns in *Montessori Architecture*.

The Ngabobo project is fully funded to completion and its progress will be documented as part of the ongoing *Montessori Architecture* project.

Tropical zone

Primary and Secondary School Gando, Burkina Faso

Subject	Primary and secondary school	Total area	13,000 m²
Design	Diébédo Francis Kéré	Open area	11,420 m²
Year	2008	Footprint area	1,580 m²
Climate	Tropical zone	Gross floor area	1,570 m²
		Classrooms/Workshops	6/0
		Number of students	—

Gando village is located in the Centre-Est Region of Burkina Faso, about 14 kilometres west by northwest of the provincial capital Tenkodogo. The climate is generally hot, with an average temperature of 36 to 40°C and unreliable rains across different seasons.

There was no school in Gando when the architect Diébédo Kéré was growing up there. The son of the village chief, he was sent away for his education at the age of seven. A scholarship from the German government took him to Berlin, where he became the first child from the village to earn a university degree. Friends in Germany helped to raise money for a school and the Burkina Faso government granted additional funds. Upon his return home, Kéré organised the community to realise the project. Men, women and children of Gando acquired the necessary skills and engaged in building the school. Children gathered stones for foundations and women brought water for the brick manufacturing. In this way, traditional building techniques were utilised alongside new engineering methods to produce a high-quality modern building, while construction and maintenance were simplified to suit the workers' capacities.

The first part of the primary school opened in October 2001 and received the Aga Khan Award for Architecture in 2004. Since then, an extension to the primary school, teachers' housing and a secondary school have been built in order to meet the growing demand for educational resources. A school library and a women's centre are currently under construction.

Whenever it rains in the region, it comes down as a torrent and many homes are swept away in periodical deluges. With this in mind, Kéré decided to set the buildings on raised platforms using stones from the vicinity. In contrast to the low houses in the surrounding area, these platforms give the school a dignified appearance and provide popular terraces for children to overlook the scenery. [Pat. 02]

Because of the minimal resources available, clay and mud were primarily used for the walls and ceilings. Clay is abundantly available in the region and is traditionally used in the construction of housing. These traditional clay-building techniques have been modified and modernised in order to create a more structurally robust construction in the form of compressed earth bricks (CEB). Earth bricks have the added advantage of being relatively easy to manufacture and also provide thermal protection in the hot climate. [Pat. 03]

To avoid the risk of erosion, the walls are protected from damaging rains with large overhanging corrugated sheet roofing. Many houses in Burkina Faso are covered with corrugated metal sheets which conduct heat from the sun into the interior living space making it intolerably hot. In this case the roofing structure separates the roofing from the clay ceiling structure, allowing for cooling airflow which draws air through the perforated ceiling clay bricks from the rooms below.

The three buildings – the primary school, the library and the secondary school – frame a rectangular courtyard open to the south-east. Each classroom has its own entrance from the courtyard. In the morning the facades and doors, facing the arriving students and teachers, are bathed in morning light, providing a welcoming entrance imparting positive energy. [Pats. 4/5]

125

Planted with huge deciduous trees, the courtyard provides a shaded area throughout the day. There are dedicated window seats outside the classrooms, where students can sit and enjoy the relative coolness of the schoolyard. Because of the cooling effect, all doors and windows in this direction are kept open during lessons, which generates the pleasing atmosphere of one big interconnected space amongst all the classrooms. Even with open windows and doors there is no acoustic interference due to the sound-absorbing quality of the thick clay walls and ceilings. Pats. 01/06/15

To keep the immense heat of the solar radiation outside, all openings are equipped with shutters. Daylight enters the rooms through the gap between the metal roof and clay ceilings, which makes the earth walls shine in a soft natural light from above. Inside, artificial electric lighting is powered by solar panels situated on the roof. Pats. 16/17

A school class consists of around sixty children. Door handles and windows are set at the level of children so all ages are able to unlatch and close openings without help. The school operates with meagre financial resources so the children are engaged with keeping the environment clean and tidy. Children are involved in wiping floors, cleaning toilets, fetching water, preparing food, doing the dishes and gardening. Pat. 09

Furniture and building elements have been sized to enable independent use by children. In this regard, it is extremely helpful that the school does provide access to water through an easy-to-use groundwater pump, as well as toilets specifically for children. Pats. 18/19

However, Diébédo Kéré's school also satisfies the need for places where students can just relax and play unobserved. One of the favoured spots is a small amphitheatre sunken into one of the terraces and shielded from the sun by the roof. Another is the sports field, where children play ball in the protecting shade of a group of trees. Pats. 22/23

To the west of the new building a location is destined to become a school garden. Whilst not yet implemented, it will eventually be cultivated to yield fruit and vegetables to be sold at the local market, creating an opportunity for real economics to be included in the school syllabus. Pat. 26

With the realisation of the garden the distribution of architectural elements will be complete, designed to respond to the daily path of the sun. While the doors of the primary and secondary schools are oriented to the sunrise, the teachers' houses are located precisely opposite, allowing not only students but also teachers to approach a luminous school in the morning. In the cooler evening, when the descending sun allows physically more intense activities such as gardening or playing football, it is the west side garden and the sports field which catch the last sun of day.

Floor Plan

0 1 3 5 10 20 m 1:400

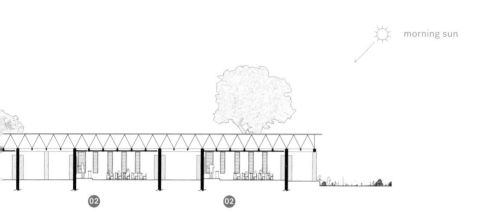

morning sun

02   02

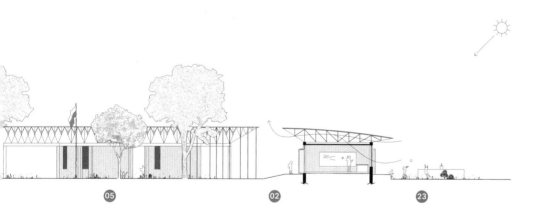

05   02   23

Sections

evening sun

A–A

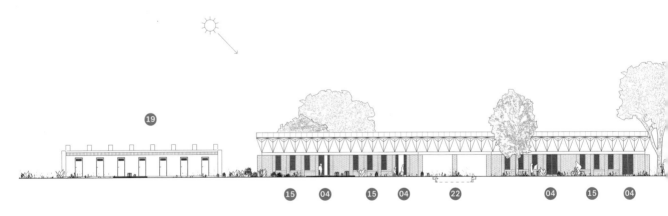

B–B

0 1 3 5   10   20 m   1:400

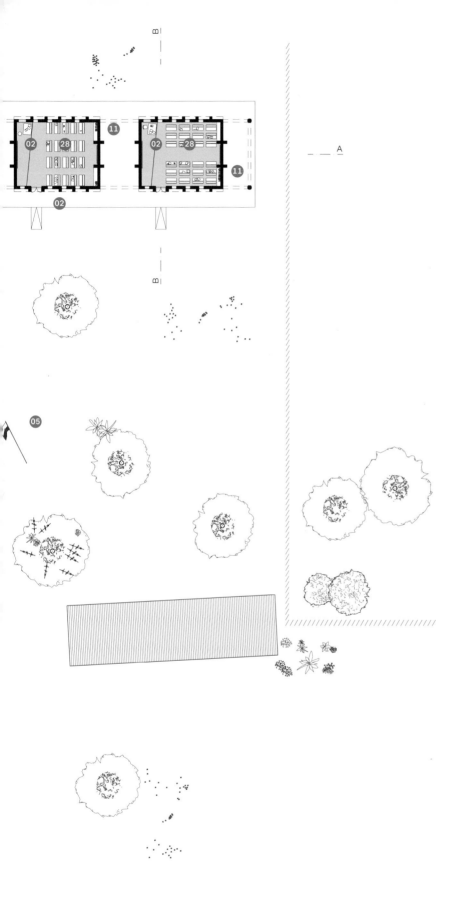

Pat. 03 ↗p. 54
Use of indigenous
materials ...

Pat. 15 ↗p. 84
Creation of window
seats ...

Pat. 16 ↗p. 88
Importance of daylight ...

134

Pat. 02 ↗ p. 52
Different heights for
floors and ceilings ...

Pat. 03 ↗ p. 54
Use of indigenous
materials ...

Pat. 09 ↗p. 70
Accessibility for
children …

Pat. 18 ↗p. 92
Meaningful access
to water …

Pat. 03 ↗p. 54
Use of indigenous
materials ...

Pat. 16 ↗p. 88
Importance of daylight ...

Pat. 18 ↗p. 92
Meaningful access
to water ...

METI Primary School
Rudrapur, Bangladesh

Subject	Primary school	Total area	4,320 m²
Design	Anna Heringer, Eike Roswag	Open area	4,045 m²
		Footprint area	275 m²
Year	2006	Gross floor area	435 m²
Climate	Tropical zone	Classrooms/Workshops	5/0
		Number of students	168

The METI (Modern Education and Training Institute) Primary School is in the village of Rudrapur located in the Dinajpur district of Bangladesh, about 290 kilometres north by northwest of Dhaka. The district lies in a tropical wet and dry climate zone with distinct monsoonal seasons. Annual temperatures average 25 °C, varying between 18 °C in January and 29 °C in August.

In 1997, Anna Heringer from Bavaria in southern Germany worked as a volunteer for the local NGO, Dipshikha, which assists marginalised communities in areas such as education, agriculture or women's health. After studying architecture at the University of Linz, Heringer again visited the village in 2004, maintaining the contacts she had enjoyed over the years. Unable to find suitable local expertise, Dipshikha appointed her as an architect to build new classrooms for the village school, with a mandate to make use of local materials. Anna Heringer began her involvement by coordinating fundraising with the German NGO, Shanti, which had initially introduced her to Dipshikha, successfully raising the funds needed for the project.

Potential exists for developing the building sector in the Rudrapur area because of the abundance of labour and locally available raw materials such as compacted earth and bamboo. The project's main strategy was to use the resource of knowledge and skills within the local population. Almost all the work was done by local labourers who acquired new skills in the process. Amongst the workers, the students took part in the construction and today they are also responsible for cleaning and maintaining the building. Historical construction methods were developed and the skills passed on to local tradesmen – in this way transforming the misconception that traditional building techniques were outdated. [Pat. 03]

The construction was completed over a period of four months from September to December 2005. As an example of sustainable architecture, the project received the Aga Khan Award for Architecture in 2007. Since then, a training centre with workshops for the teaching of technical skills to older students has been implemented, using the same design and building technique. [Pat. 27]

The METI is not a Montessori school but offers an alternative child-directed work approach rather than the conventional frontal classroom approach to lessons. The two-storey architecture of the new school reflects this principle and provides different kinds of spaces for children to work.

On the ground floor are three classrooms, each of which has an entrance located along the eastern perimeter. The upper floor is accessible through a central staircase again open to the east. The specific orientation of doors and stairway generates a magnificent view in the morning, as students and teachers enter the school lit by the morning sun. The building majestically sits on a stone base which also acts as a veranda and which is the place where pupils line up their shoes, sandals and slippers. The ground floor, which is built with thick earth walls, is dedicated to the younger children. The three classrooms have their own openings onto an organically shaped system of 'caves' to the rear of the building. The soft interiors of theses caves are for retreating, for exploration or concentration, on one's own or in a group. [Pats. 04/11/14]

143

In contrast to the protective massiveness of the ground floor, the upper deck is open and airy, made of a light bamboo construction covered with corrugated metal sheets. The large interior provides a huge connected space for free movement and learning areas for older students. [Pat. 01]

In the upper floor, the walls have openings with shades made of woven bamboo which can be opened or closed to control the amount of air and sun entering the room. A spectacular bamboo balcony offers a sweeping view across the treetops and the village pond. When the shades are closed, air still flows in and out through the gaps while solar heat radiation is mostly blocked. The gaps also let in daylight, and even when most of the shades are closed enough light comes into the classroom.

The bamboo construction rests on a surrounding parapet, which also acts as an attractive window seat. The parapet also satisfies the need for a certain degree of seclusion for students working on the floor. [Pats. 8/15]

One of the most striking characteristics of the METI school is the absence of any furniture, with chart boards and chairs for the teachers as the only exceptions. Students work, play and even eat on the floor mats, sometimes using the parapet as a backrest. [Pats. 08/09/28]

Self-reliance is encouraged, with children moderating the environment with the bamboo screen doors; they also have access to water at will from a child-sized groundwater pump installed in the schoolyard. The toilets are located in a separate building slightly apart from the school and the unattended walk from the classroom, across the schoolyard, creates a variety of interactions and on occasion contemplation. [Pats. 09/18/19]

Both, the METI school and the training centre provide a garden where students grow flowers, vegetables and fruit. In addition, there are two sports fields located on the west and the east side of the school. Related to the position of the sun, the east field is mainly for volleyball games in the morning while the west field is occupied by girls and boys from the afternoon until sunset. [Pat. 23]

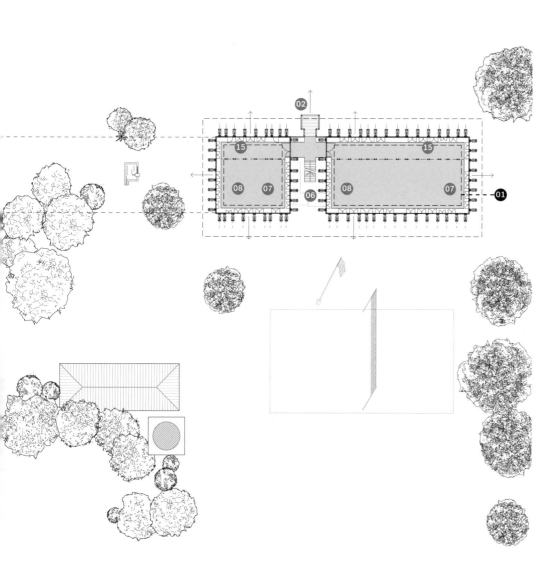

Upper Floor

Sections

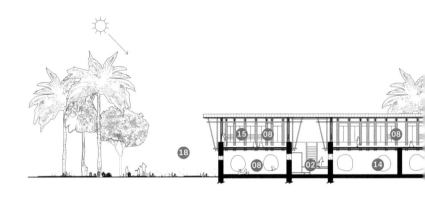

A–A

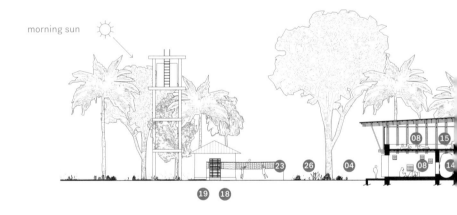

B–B

0 1 3 5   10   20 m   1:400

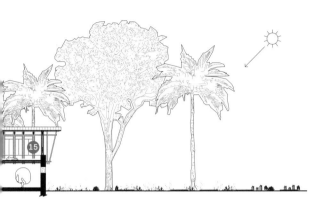

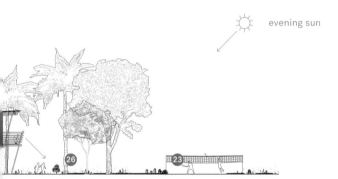

evening sun

Floor Plans

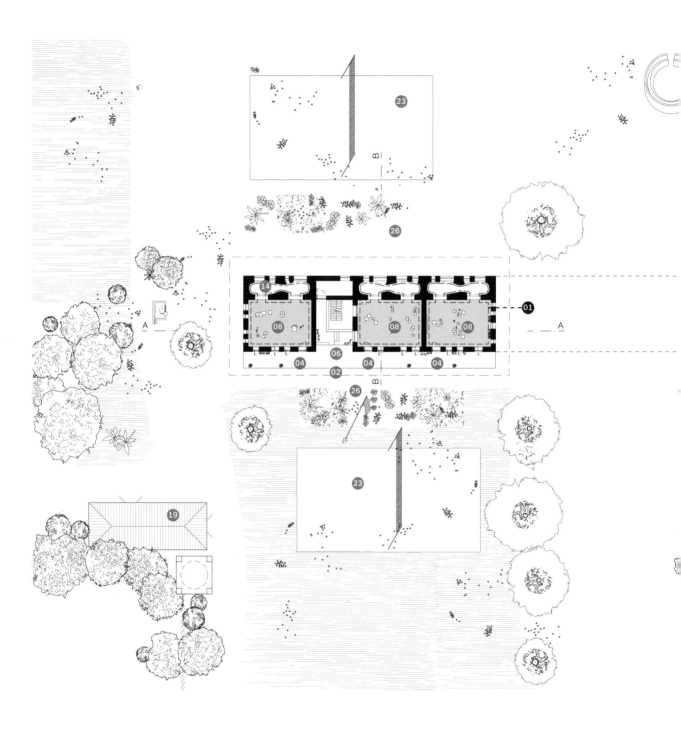

Ground Floor

0 1 3 5   10   20 m   1:400

149

Pat. 02 ↗p. 52
Different heights for
floors and ceilings …

Pat. 03 ↗p. 54
Use of indigenous
materials …

Pat. 05 ↗p. 60
Connecting function
of the greeting space …

Pat. 03 ↗p. 54
Use of indigenous
materials ...

Pat. 04 ↗p. 58
Orientation of the
entrance ...

152

Pat. 01 ↗ p. 50
A hierarchy of
interconnected spaces ...

Pat. 03 ↗ p. 54
Use of indigenous
materials ...

Pat. 06 ↗ p. 62
Avoidance of doors ...

Pat. 03 ↗p. 54
Use of indigenous
materials …

Pat. 05 ↗p. 60
Connecting function
of the greeting space …

Pat. 22 ↗p. 102
Everyday gathering
spaces ...

St. Bridget's Montessori School
Colombo, Sri Lanka

Subject	**Children's House**	Total area	**1,728 m²**
Design	**Geoffrey Bawa**	Open area	**462 m²**
Year	**1964**	Footprint area	**1,266 m²**
Climate	**Tropical zone**	Gross floor area	**1,363 m²**
		Classrooms/Workshops	**2/0**
		Number of students	**200**

This Montessori school was built in the grounds of the St. Bridget's Convent in Colombo in the 1960s. Sri Lanka features a tropical monsoon climate, fairly temperate throughout the year. From March to April the average high temperature is around 31 °C. The only major change in the weather occurs during the monsoon seasons with heavy rainfall from May to August and October to January. Rainfall in the city averages around 2,500 millimetres per year.

The Sri Lankan architect Geoffrey Bawa, together with the local artist Laki Senanayake, reworked traditional 'wattle-and-daub' village schools to develop the design of a rounded, rectangular two-storey building. Bawa's architecture was generally rooted in the traditions of functional Modernism and, despite his admiration for the Baroque and his love of decoration, he rarely strayed into the realms of Expressionism. Here, however, the skeletal structure, the organic forms and the naive decorative patterns are reminiscent of Gaudí's Park Güell in Barcelona.

The school was completed in 1964 and is still in almost pristine condition even after fifty-four years of constant use, though some additions and repainting may have disturbed the harmonies of the original design.

The entrance to the compound is set on the east. In the morning, parents drop off their children in front of a gate which reflects beautifully the golden colour of the first daylight. Guardians are not allowed to step through the doorway and the positive image of the shining gate welcomes the children. In the covered greeting space between the gate and the school, girls and boys wave goodbye to their relatives. Pats. 04/05

Basically, the school consists of two huge open spaces, one on each storey connected by spiral staircases on either end. A surrounding terrace and the staircases are cast in rough, curving concrete in a manner that is reminiscent of traditional rammed earth constructions. Used by several classes at the same time, there is no room separation and subsequently no internal doors. Teaching areas are delineated by low walls and child-sized shelves that create small-scale enclosures within the megastructure of the roof and the floor slab. The low walls are thick enough to offer additional storages for each enclosure. Pats. 01/02/06/07/09/11

The upper floor is covered by a huge umbrella of Portuguese tiles on cement sheeting that cantilevers far out beyond the perimeter of the classroom to protect the interior from driving rain and harsh sunlight. In some parts, translucent roofing sheets bring in light from the top, supporting the articulation of some special places such as the Walking on the Line space in the centre of the upper floor. Rafters are elegantly supported by an interlocked concrete frame. The upper-floor slab sits on mushroom-topped columns and its soffit is modelled to create a cave-like quality. Pats. 16/24

Despite the huge overhanging roof, the ground floor was periodically affected by cloudbursts, making teaching almost impossible during monsoon seasons. Due to this, glass fronts have been installed, eliminating the open-air atmosphere which still is apparent in the upper floor. There, the open sides and the high roof encourage natural ventilation and the surrounding vegetation helps to cool the air. Students and teachers are embedded in the soundscape of the town's neighbourhood – singing birds, the motor traffic, the melodious chant of a Hindu procession. Because they are visually screened off by a parapet, with small openings and decorative features, pupils feel protected and, at the same time, still a part of their world. Pats. 10/20

Originally, Bawa had installed toilets in freestanding concrete chambers with organic shapes that suggested hollowed-out boulders. These chambers were removed because they did not offer any natural light or fresh air and came to be avoided by the children. Instead, open-air toilets have been installed at the tip of both storeys, enclosed only by low walls and half doors, the new compartments allow the teacher to keep an eye on the children whilst respecting the need for privacy. Pats. 13/19

The removal of the concrete chambers created empty floor space now used by pupils as additional worktops and playground. In addition, it provided the possibility to install ensembles of freestanding sinks guaranteeing quick access to potable water – for drinking, washing and cleaning – from any point in the school. Pats. 08/18

With the exception of the shelves, a group of small tables and stools, there is very little other furniture to be found in the St. Bridget's Montessori School. Predominately, children choose to work on mats which they put on the floor. A favourite workplace is at one of the small wooden tables in front of a low part of the parapet, which captures the view of the greenery of the garden. Pats. 08/15

From the ground floor, children have free access to the garden and open-air playground, located to the west of the school. After lunch, when students feel slightly tired, they find recreational equipment such as seesaws swings or slides. In addition, there is an aviary that protects local birds that have become extremely rare in Colombo. Pats. 23/25/26

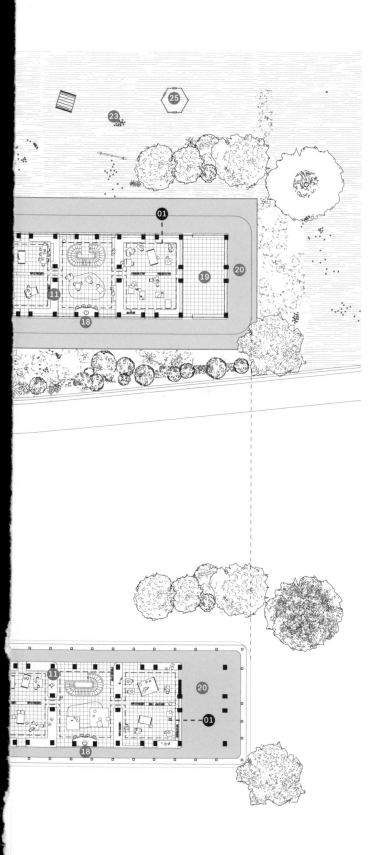

Sections

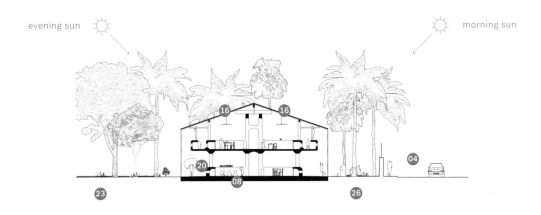

evening sun

morning sun

A–A

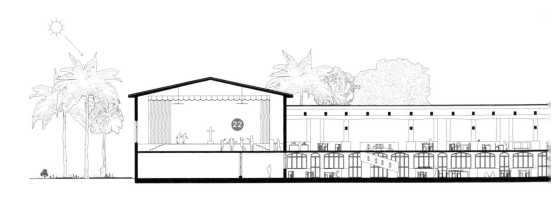

B–B

0 1 3   5   10   20 m   1:400

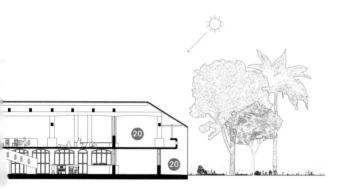

Floor Plans

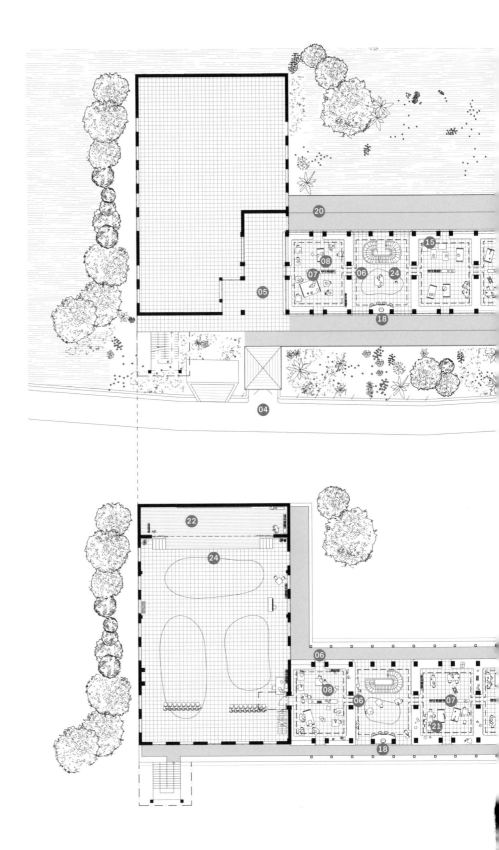

Ground Floor

Upper Floor

0 1 3 5   10   20 m   1:400

Pat. 20 ↗p. 96
Transitional spaces be-
tween inside and outside ...

Pat. 04 ↗ p. 58
Orientation of the
entrance...

Pat. 01 ↗p. 50
A hierarchy of
interconnected spaces …

Pat. 07 ↗p. 66
Articulation of space
and form …

Pat. 08 ↗p. 68
Use of the floor as
a primary workplace

Pat. 03 ↗p. 54
Use of indigenous
materials …

Pat. 06 ↗p. 62
Avoidance of doors …

Pat. 10 ↗p. 72
Consideration of the
acoustical environment …

Pat. 09 ↗p. 70
Accessibility for children …

Pat. 18 ↗p. 92
Meaningful access
to water …

Pat. 01 ↗p. 50
A hierarchy of
interconnected spaces ...

Pat. 07 ↗p. 66
Articulation of space and
form ...

Pat. 12 ↗p. 78
Open storage and display
of learning materials

Pat. 16 ↗ p. 88
Importance of daylight ...

Simba Vision Montessori Campus, Ngabobo, Tanzania

Subject	Children's House and primary school	Total area	13,329 m²
		Open area	10,340 m²
Design	APC Architectural Pioneering Consultants	Footprint area	2,989 m²
		Gross floor area	4,829 m²
Year	2022	Classrooms/Workshops	10/2
Climate	Tropical zone	Number of students	720

Ngabombo Village is located in Tanzania's remote northern savanna, just three degrees south of the equator. Having a subtropical highland climate with mild annual temperatures ranging between 18 and 23°C, the plains between Mt Meru and Mt Kilimanjaro lie at an altitude of approximately 1,100 m. The mountainous landscape sets the breathtaking backdrop of this project. These plains are inhabited by Meru and Maasai communities, tribes which are currently slowly shifting from a traditional, semi-nomadic lifestyle based on herding cattle to a life in permanent settlements, with irrigated agriculture and motorised transportation.

In 2019, Africa Amini Alama, a local NGO which has been active in healthcare and education, called for a design competition to develop one of their existing schools into a Montessori campus consisting of an additional primary school, Children's House, workshops and dormitories for students and teachers. Partnering with the Arthur Waser Foundation, the occasion was used as an opportunity to test a first prototype of this twenty-eight-pattern 'Design Instrument'. [Pat. 27]

Dar es Salaam-based APC (Architectural Pioneering Consultants) submitted the winning proposal. The team had been successful because they best incorporated the *Montessori Architectural Patterns* in correspondence with the environmental and sociocultural values of the Maasai area. The twenty-eight patterns led to a number of notable key decisions, which, in turn, fit seamlessly with the conditions of the place and the needs of the community.

The remote location of the site, and the ambition to operate with an ecologically low impact, led to a simple block wall construction, which consists of volcanic rock and sand, naturally available on site in an ideal mix. Blocks consist of only 10 per cent of cement and without the need for additional reinforcement. Interior spaces are partly clad with straw and mud to improve comfort and acoustics, a technique traditionally carried out by Maasai women. The use of steel is reserved for the roof, which acts as a sunshade and rainwater harvester. The mild year-round climate allows for the building to operate without mechanical cooling or heating and with a minimum of artificial but activity-based lighting. A combination of natural ventilation, sun shading and thermal mass ensure thermal comfort. [Pats. 03/10/17]

As a reaction to the harsh winds and the natural orientation of the site, the buildings are arranged in two parallel north–south alignments, with a roofed entrance from the east, between the workshop and Children's House. The two strings of buildings form a tree-shaded greeting space dominated by a large sunken amphitheatre. Separate toilet buildings on both ends of the open space can be reached by a short stroll under the trees and alongside the theatre. A stream flowing along the site's western perimeter provides water to the small farm run by teachers and pupils. A line of unusually large trees at the fringe of the stream resonates with the building's orientation and height. [Pats. 04/19/22]

Unique for the area, the Simba Vision buildings develop over more than one storey. A few steps up mark the plinths of the houses, which, like an artificial topography of natural stones, stretch into the entrance halls with raised ceilings. Inside the learning spaces, further steps lead up to the adjacent niches, where lower ceiling heights create appropriate spatial proportions. Steps between different levels are designed to be sat, played and worked on. The entrance halls and staircases become versatile spaces for social interaction and learning. As a spatial attraction, two-storey open shelves for books and learning materials are embedded into the entrance walls. Pats. 02/05/08/11/12/22

From the open-air greeting space with the theatre down to the snug reading niches, students and teachers enjoy a range of public and private, common and individual, exposed and sheltered places. Along with the design and construction of the school buildings, the provision of potable water was arranged, too. Wall fountains are distributed in every room. The children's kitchen with its outside food preparation area includes the children in the processes of cooking, serving, washing up and cleaning. Pats. 09/14/15/18/21

In the interior, a series of connected but specific spaces characterise the school. The walls are rotated at an angle of 45° to the main orientation of the structures and clearly identify every room as a distinct space already from outside. The geometry of 45° angles creates an array of visually protected corners, whereby the individual users of these corners form smaller groups within the class community. Rooms are aligned like pearls on a string without the need for typical corridors and can therefore be connected according to programmatic needs. Connection between rooms can be gradually opened or closed through generously proportioned sliding doors. Pats. 01/06/07/13

Buildings allow for free circulation from outside and within, encouraging interaction between the interior and exterior garden areas. Transitions are designed to be gradual, taking full advantage of the mild climate. At all entrances the plinth protrudes towards the surroundings, forming transitional terraces for a variety of activities. The large roof overhang further blurs the border between buildings and landscape, providing sheltered outdoor spaces and drawing visitors from the open spaces into its shade. Pats. 20/26

The school campus has no fenced perimeter. Paths leading to the main entrances and the greetings space fade out into the landscape where the number of children walking on them gradually diminish. A large football pitch and playing area on the eastern plot boundary forms a spatial counterpart to the children's gardens and stables, opposite. Pats. 23/25

Construction of the Simba Vision Montessori Campus started in 2020. The completion of the first learning spaces is anticipated to coincide with the publication of this book.

Floor Plans

First Floor

Ground Floor

0 1 3 5   10   20 m   1:400

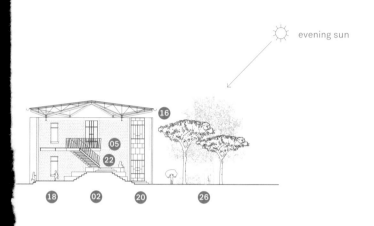

evening sun

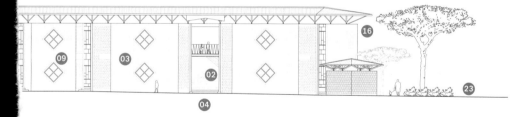

Sections

morning sun

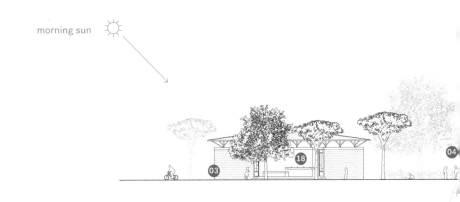

A-A

B-B

0 1 3 5   10   20 m   1:400

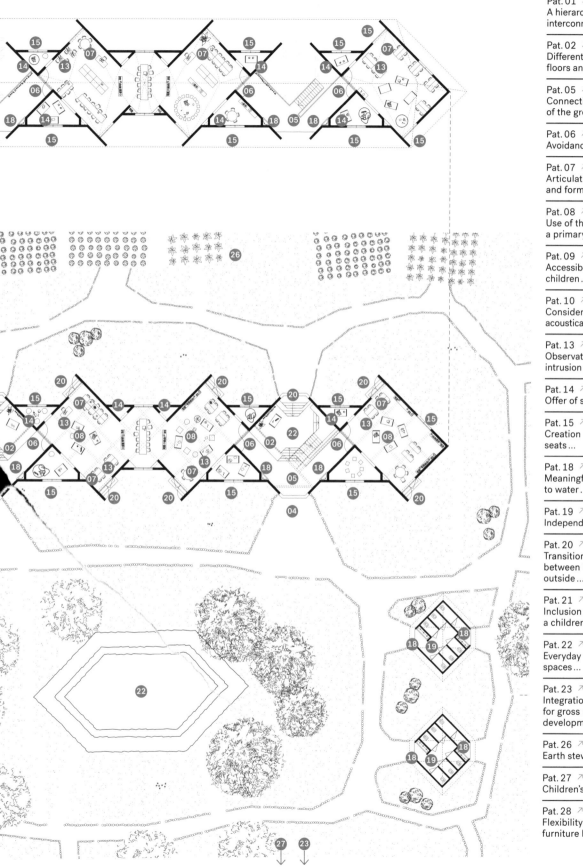

Pat. 02 ↗p. 52
Different heights for floors
and ceilings ...

Pat. 06 ↗p. 62
Avoidance of doors ...

Pat. 16 ↗p. 88
Importance of daylight ...

Pat. 03 ↗p. 54
Use of indigenous
materials ...

Pat. 04 ↗p. 58
Orientation of the
entrance ...

Pat. 22 ↗p. 102
Everyday gathering
spaces ...

Pat. 03 ↗p. 54
Use of indigenous
materials ...

Pat. 15 ↗p. 84
Creation of window
seats ...

Pat. 20 ↗p. 96
Transitional spaces be-
tween inside and outside ...

Pat. 02 ↗p. 52
Different heights for floors
and ceilings …

Pat. 03 ↗p. 54
Use of indigenous
materials …

Pat. 04 ↗p. 58
Orientation of the
entrance …

Pat. 15 ↗p. 84
Creation of window
seats ...

Pat. 20 ↗p. 96
Transitional spaces be-
tween inside and outside ...

Pat. 22 ↗p. 102
Everyday gathering
spaces ...

Pat. 01 ↗ p. 50
A hierarchy of
interconnected spaces ...

Pat. 03 ↗ p. 54
Use of indigenous
materials ...

Pat. 06 ↗ p. 62
Avoidance of doors ...

Temperate zone

Amsterdamse Montessori School (Apollo Schools)
Amsterdam, the Netherlands

Subject	Secondary school	Total area	3,070 m²
Design	Herman Hertzberger,	Open area	2,575 m²
	Henk de Weijer,	Footprint area	495 m²
	Jan Rietvink	Gross floor area	1,357 m²
Year	1983	Classrooms/Workshops	8/1
Climate	Temperate zone	Number of students	120

In the 1980s, the Dutch architect Herman Hertzberger was commissioned by the City of Amsterdam to design two schools at the corner of Apollolaan and Willem Witsenstraat. One was to be a conventional elementary school and the other was to be a Montessori school. The two schools are known as the Apollo Schools. The constrained building site, beautifully situated in a spacious green area, inspired Hertzberger to create two villa-style buildings, in harmony with the large detached houses in the neighbourhood. In spite of two different educational systems, the two schools were developed from the same principles like identical twins. The schools are constructed with locally produced concrete blocks (a typical material for Hertzberger's buildings) and are based on an identical scheme in which the classrooms, one in each corner of a square, are grouped around a central hall. By introducing a variation in the detailing, the architect has given each school its own identity.

Hertzberger's interest in educational architecture, in particular Montessori, goes back to his own school days as a Montessori child from the age of four until eighteen. Not only is he married to a Montessori teacher but one of his daughters is also a Montessori teacher and he is unique in having attended the same Montessori school as Renilde Montessori, Maria's granddaughter, and at the age of four meeting Maria Montessori herself. Hertzberger's natural respect for the children as the 'owners' of their school can be recognised in his tendency to refer to 'people' or 'users' and he only occasionally refers to children.

The main entrance to the schoolyard is set on the east side, so each day the children and their parents approach the school grounds facing the positive image of the facades lit by the morning sun. Both schools have been positioned so that the schoolyard is divided into a semi-public section and a more sheltered part, which has been specially designed for small children. While older students enter the buildings through the exterior stairways, infants have their own access on the ground floor beneath. Pats. 03/04

The first impression of the interior fits with the image of a noble villa. Crowned with a massive skylight window, the heart of the school is a light-filled open greeting space which connects all the classrooms on four different storeys to one interconnected space. In order to regulate the contact between classrooms and hall as subtly as possible, half doors have been installed, offering the right degree of openness towards the hall as well as the required seclusion from it. The entrance to each classroom encompasses a 'wardrobe' area with coat and shoe racks and there is a display case next to every doorway. Pats. 01/02/06/16

With an amphitheatre-like organisation, which includes sight lines from the galleries and the stair, Hertzberger has created, within a central atrium volume, an assembly space for official or spontaneous gatherings, big enough to accommodate the entire school if necessary. Plywood is the chosen material for the amphitheatre steps and, combined with their very shape and form, a naturally inviting workplace is created. The dense building materials, the wooden surfaces and the complex geometry of the atrium prevent echoes and enable a pleasing acoustic atmosphere despite the large open volume. Pats. 03/10/22

197

The central meeting space also represents extensions of the classrooms, where students can study on their own. There are several work desks with their specific activity-based lighting and benches enclosed by low walls. The children feel the trust given to work beyond the direct supervision of the teachers. On the other hand, the teachers are not entirely screened off from what happens outside the classroom. Since children were given access to computers in primary schools, these places are used as computer workstations. Pats. 05/17

Each classroom is slightly L-shaped, which helps to articulate different places in the room. Dimensions have been chosen so children can use the floor as workplace and the desks and chairs, of differing heights, which are manufactured in plywood, are mobile and light, so children are able to re-arrange them, at will, at any time. The room shape also creates corners where students can work with or without the direct oversight of the teachers, which adds to the Montessori philosophy to observe without intrusion by respecting privacy. In some of the learning spaces special nooks have been created at high level with ladder access to provide cosy bunks with a degree of seclusion for reading or napping. Pats. 07/08/13/14/28

Hertzberger has gone to the extent of designing built-in furniture, such as kitchen islands, in the middle of the rooms. In the Apollo Schools every classroom contains a freestanding cabinet with an integrated sink for washing hands, preparation of snacks, cooking or doing the dishes. Like all other furniture and building elements in the classrooms and the connecting spaces, these 'islands' are specifically designed to enable children to act independently. They also guarantee easy access to water from anywhere in the school. Pats. 09/18/21

Independent use also concerns the different toilets, each sized and dedicated to a particular age group. Half doors and glass bricks between the toilets and the classrooms satisfy just the right degree of visual obscurity while allowing a certain oversight by the teachers. Shelves are open and the educational materials are arranged in an ordered and inviting manner. This allows the individual child to choose freely and to put back the material in its right place without the adult's help – everything to enhance the self-confidence and autonomy of the children. Pats. 12/19

Windowsills are generally deep, providing ledges for the children to keep plants, and at ground floor level the windowsill is designed as a step-up giving access out into the garden. In this way, the huge classroom windows not only offer a breathtaking view of the schoolyard or neighbourhood but also provide a strong connection between the classrooms and the biological environment. There is a plant on every desk for which the individual student is responsible. Pat. 25

In the afternoon, when the human metabolism may feel some fatigue, the smaller children on the ground floor find special exits to the sand-pits and little garden to engage themselves in more physical activities. For the older students on the upper floors, the Apollo Schools offer workshops for handicrafts, such as painting, modelling, sewing or carpentry. Therefore, garden, sandpits and workshop are all located on the west side, so they catch the sun in the afternoon and evening. Pats. 26/27

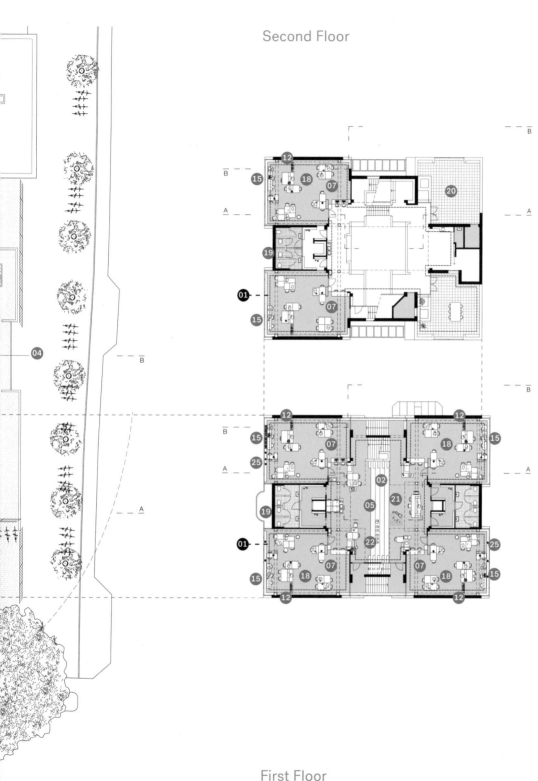

Second Floor

First Floor

Sections

evening sun

A–A

B–B

0 1   3   5   10   20 m   1:400

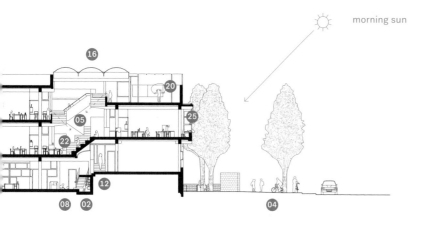

morning sun

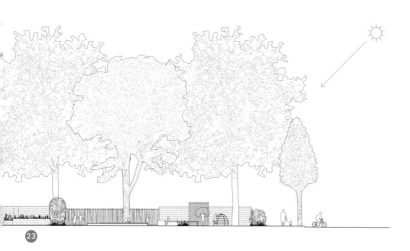

Floor Plans

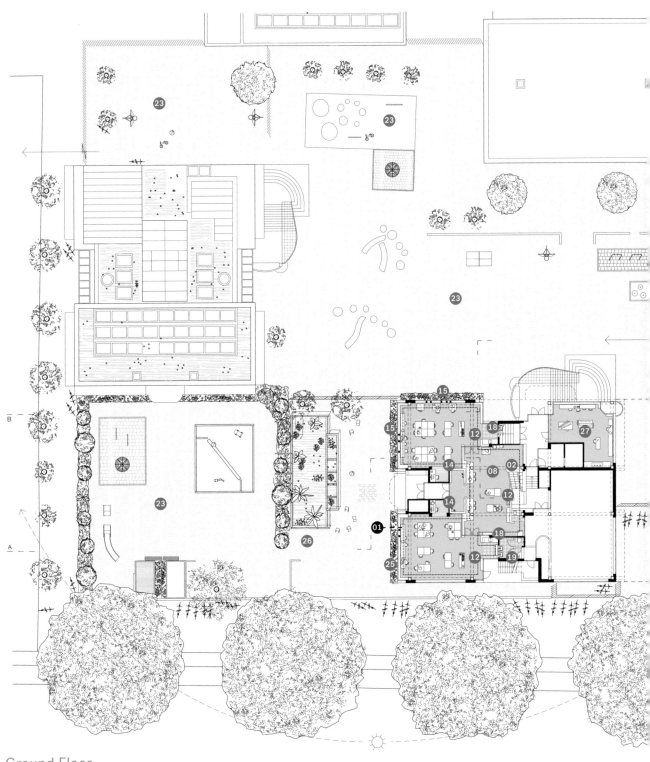

Ground Floor

0 1 3   5   10   20 m   1:400

Pat. 26 ↗p. 110
Earth stewardship ...

Pat. 01 ↗ p. 50
A hierarchy of
interconnected spaces ...

Pat. 02 ↗ p. 52
Different heights for
floors and ceilings ...

Pat. 03 ↗ p. 54
Use of indigenous
materials ...

Pat. 03 ↗p. 54
Use of indigenous
materials ...

Pat. 14 ↗p. 82
Offer of seclusion ...

Pat. 28 ↗p. 114
Flexibility in
furniture layout

Pat. 03 ↗p. 54
Use of indigenous
materials ...

Pat. 18 ↗p. 92
Meaningful access
to water ...

Stichting Casa School
Pijnacker, Rotterdam,
the Netherlands

Subject	Children's House and primary school	Total area	4,520 m²
		Open area	3,020 m²
Design	Tessa Wessels	Footprint area	1,500 m²
Year	2011	Gross floor area	1,494 m²
Climate	Temperate zone	Classrooms/Workshops	6/1
		Number of students	250

The Pijnacker Casa School was created in 2011 as an Algemeen Bijzonder (literally, a general special) school in response to a popular demand for a Montessori school in this residential area in the suburbs of Rotterdam. Dutch law requires the state to provide buildings and teachers for a school for which popular demand exists and which can be shown to have the prospect of growing to 400 children and being sustainable thereafter.

The Pijnacker site is the second location for the school, which very quickly outgrew its original location. The building is provided by the state and has been reconfigured as a Montessori school for children from ages three to twelve. Amongst the underpinning concepts for the school is an 'All Day, All Year' concept to allow flexible school care and holiday times to suit the population of working parents. A bilingual approach is taken in both Dutch and English and the idea of the child working 'in and with nature' is a central theme in this urban location.

The school building is a repurposed single-storey building, constructed in brick with full-height timber-framed panel windows. It has a flat roof with concealed gutters and the floor is concrete covered with a variety of surfaces including linoleum, veneered engineered boards, ceramic tiles and carpets. There is a conventional hot water radiator heating system and the large south-facing windows have shading blinds.

The school building is configured around and within three main articulated external spaces, an east-facing entrance garden and play area, a central almost fully enclosed courtyard and a vegetable garden. The entire building is set back from the boundary and an informal path meanders around the building connecting the three articulated spaces.

Entrance to the school is through a garden gate into the east-facing entrance garden, which has bicycle racks on its southern perimeter. Steps and a ramp lead to the east-facing front door and greeting area, which immediately opens through to the central courtyard around which three of the six classrooms are arranged. [Pat. 04]

The entrance hall opens onto a dining area and kitchen. An east-west passageway from the entrance hall along the south side of the courtyard connects two classrooms for three- to six-year-olds and a dedicated gymnasium. [Pats. 05/23]

The courtyard itself contains an open-air children's workshop and housing for chickens and rabbits. A second passage from the entrance hall leads north to a classroom for six- to nine-year-olds on the north side of the main courtyard and then turns left to the east to connect two further classrooms, for ages six to nine and nine to twelve. This passage has windows onto a northeast garden which is laid out with a productive vegetable section and at the eastern end is equipped with a children's kitchen. [Pats. 21/25/27]

All of the six classrooms open out onto the external spaces and, whilst the modest building construction is a constraining factor, the resulting form and reconfiguration as a Montessori school have made it complex and interesting. [Pat. 01]

Pat. 17 ↗ p. 90
Activity-based
lighting...

Colour is introduced in the form of one brightly painted wall in each of the classrooms. Daylight is abundant because of the ceiling-height windows in every classroom; it is supplemented by background lighting panels fitted into the suspended ceiling system and sculptural hanging lights. [Pat. 17]

216

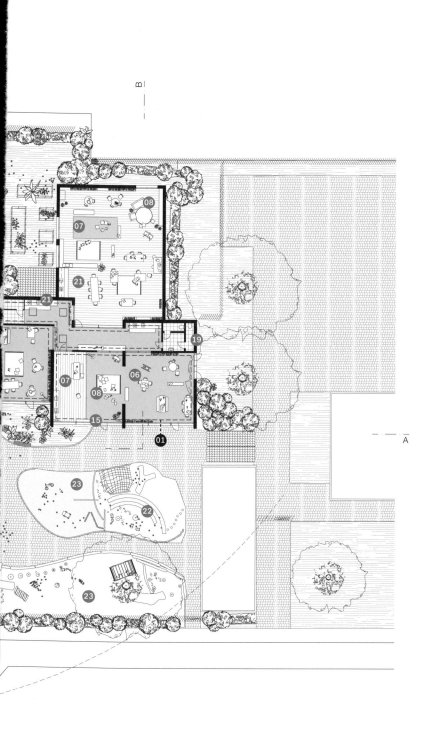

Sections

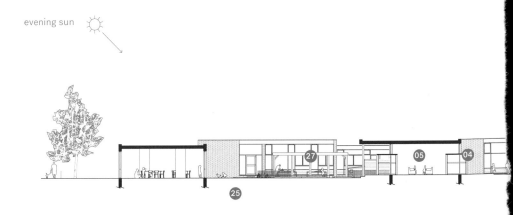

evening sun

A–A

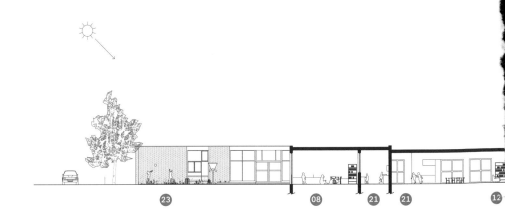

B–B

0 1 3 5   10   20 m   1:400

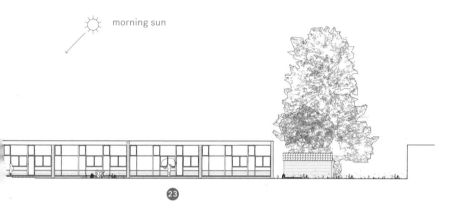

morning sun

㉓

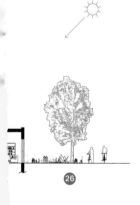

㉖

Floor Plan

Pat. 23 ↗p. 104
Integration of spaces for
gross motor development...

Pat. 03 ↗ p. 54
Use of indigenous
materials ...

Pat. 26 ↗ p. 110
Earth stewardship ...

Pat. 01 ↗p. 50
A hierarchy of
interconnected spaces …

Pat. 03 ↗p. 54
Use of indigenous
materials …

Pat. 06 ↗p. 62
Avoidance of doors …

Pat. 08 ↗p. 68
Use of the floor as
a primary workplace

Pat. 12 ↗p. 78
Open storage and display
of learning materials

Pat. 21 ↗p. 98
Inclusion of a children's
kitchen …

Pat. 03 ↗p. 54
Use of indigenous
materials ...

Pat. 06 ↗p. 62
Avoidance of doors ...

Pat. 07 ↗p. 66
Articulation of space
and form ...

Pat. 09 ↗p. 70
Accessibility for children ...

Pat. 27 ↗p. 112
Children's workshop ...

International Montessori School Hof Kleinenberg St. Stevens-Woluwe, Belgium

Subject	Children's House and primary school	Total area	6,834 m²
		Open area	5,877 m²
Design	Annie Hoekstra-de Roos, Rinze Hoekstra	Footprint area	957 m²
		Gross floor area	1,535 m²
Year	2008	Classrooms/Workshops	7/0
Climate	Temperate zone	Number of students	160

'Hof Kleinenberg' is one of a group of four locations on the east side of Brussels which are part of the International Montessori Schools, Brussels. The group of schools has grown over a period of more than twenty-five years in response to the high demand from the international community in Brussels for schools to suit children from multilingual and multicultural backgrounds.

The site at 'Hof Kleinenberg' involved the careful restoration of a historic farm dating from 1651. With respect for the environment, the renovations have been done without the use of synthetic products and included the installation of rainwater tanks to supply the school's bathrooms and gardens. Today, the location caters for children aged between two and eighteen and consists of several Children's Houses, a primary and a secondary section. Besides Montessori, the latter is aligned with the International Baccalaureate middle years and diploma programmes. The architectural development of the sites has been overseen by Annie Hoekstra-de Roos and Rinze Hoekstra. Pats. 03/18/26

The rectangular building complex consists of a tall two-storey trussed barn orientated approximately north/south with two lower ridge- height and two-storey buildings at right angles under tiled roofs forming three sides of a courtyard. The fourth side is being completed with a tall roofed wooden double gate with a wicket door. There are two car-parking areas at the east and west ends of the buildings and a road, from which vehicular access is gained, runs along the north side. Extensive land falls away to the south side.

The principal entrance is to the east, but there are also entrances on the south side through the garden and on the west side through the gates into the courtyard; this turns to an east-facing entrance for younger children, opening into a tiled greeting space with coat racks, chairs, stools and a piano for impromptu and instructional use. Pats. 04/05

The construction of the buildings is masonry with compound trusses supporting tiled roofs. The restoration was from a derelict state and incudes significant insulation, underfloor heating with red clay tiles at ground floor level, linoleum-covered suspended timber floors at first floor level, extensive new fenestration in primary green powder-coated wood and extensive use of roof lights in the large planes of tiled roof and particularly on the courtyard-facing roof elevations. The existing restored wooden compound trusses are left exposed throughout and are a defining element in establishing the character of the school at the upper level. Weaving the spaces through the existing structure has created a complex hierarchy of interconnected and multifunctional spaces. Pats. 01/03

The main barn, known as a '10% barn', was originally constructed to allow carts to run through the building and be loaded with grain stored at the upper level. Every tenth cartload was taken for tax, hence the '10% barn'. This barn forms the domain for the older children in the elementary and secondary levels. The ground floor space has two symmetric and opposing staircases rising from the entrance area either side of the front door. This open space has no divisions or doors and opens directly onto the courtyard. It has double-height space to the aisle section of the roof and roof lights bring sky light down to the lower level and create a visual connection between upper and lower levels. The furniture layout is entirely flexible, and this space also becomes the internal everyday theatre space. [Pats. 04/06/07/16/22]

Fire-resistant glass screens and doors enclose the two staircases at the upper level maintaining visual connections, but apart from these the upper barn level is a single articulated space with visual connection to the ground floor. The first floor level is formed mostly within the queen posts of the compound truss with the visual connection to the ground floor via the eaves volume beyond this framework. At the south end of the upper level is the children's kitchen and a maths area with storage shelving for the advanced maths apparatus. Triangular roof lights at a high level on the east side of the roof bring in the morning sunshine. [Pats. 16/21]

Modern demi-hexagonal and rectangular tables are distributed at will by the students around the space sometimes individually and sometimes in bigger or smaller groups. Some older and even antique furniture creates variety. Dedicated computers and printers are provided in a few locations and angle-poise lamps are available for intense task lighting. Ambient lighting is daylight supplemented with multiple ceiling spotlights. [Pat. 17]

The 10% barn opens onto the courtyard at the ground floor level and at the upper level it connects into the north and south barns through openings on the ridgeline axis and within the compound truss below the collar beam. [Pats. 01/02]

The north-side barn has been restored with roof lights at the upper level, but below the purlin line and in one part, roof lights have been inserted either side of the ridge beam exploiting the height of the space and accentuating the exposed compound roof truss structure incorporating arch-bracing and high-level king posts. The space is predominantly used by elementary level children aged from nine to twelve. Furniture placed at floor level changes and, corresponding with the rhythm of the truss structure, has created alcoves and niches and thus a variety of workplaces.

A double-height library space has been created at the west end of the north barn with bookshelves filling the entirety of its two high walls to the apex. Access to the highest level is by ladder. The lining of books reduces the acoustic reverberation time of the space, making it very tranquil. A square window on axis with the ridgeline works as a window seat and is reflected by a similar window looking over a staircase to the ground floor at this end of the building. [Pats. 02/10/11]

The ground floor of the north barn is occupied by a Children's House in two interconnected volumes. It has its own entrance and greeting space and toilets opening off the courtyard; a combined children's/adult's kitchen is included in this space. It has a window seat overlooking the courtyard and double doors opening out, too. [Pats. 05/18/19/20/21/24]

Across the courtyard, the ground floor of the south building contains two more Children's House classrooms connected through a common greeting space. Both rooms have direct access to the garden to the south.

234

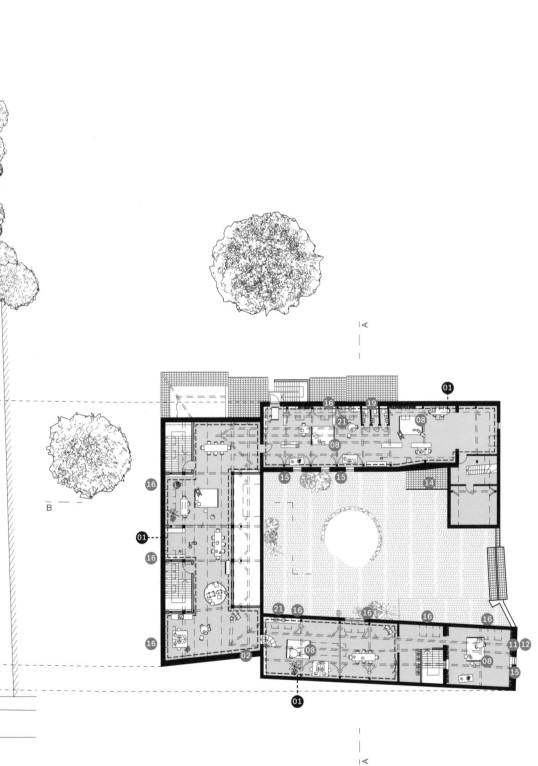

Upper Floor

Sections

A–A

morning sun

B–B

0 1 3 5   10   20 m   1:400

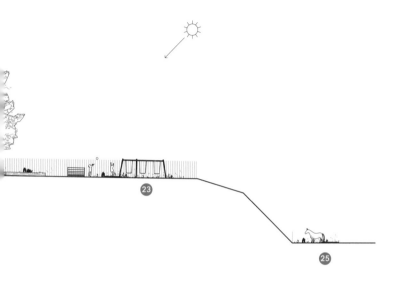

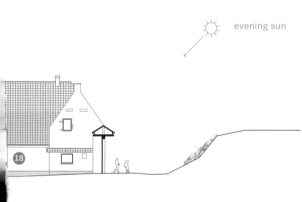

evening sun

Floor Plans

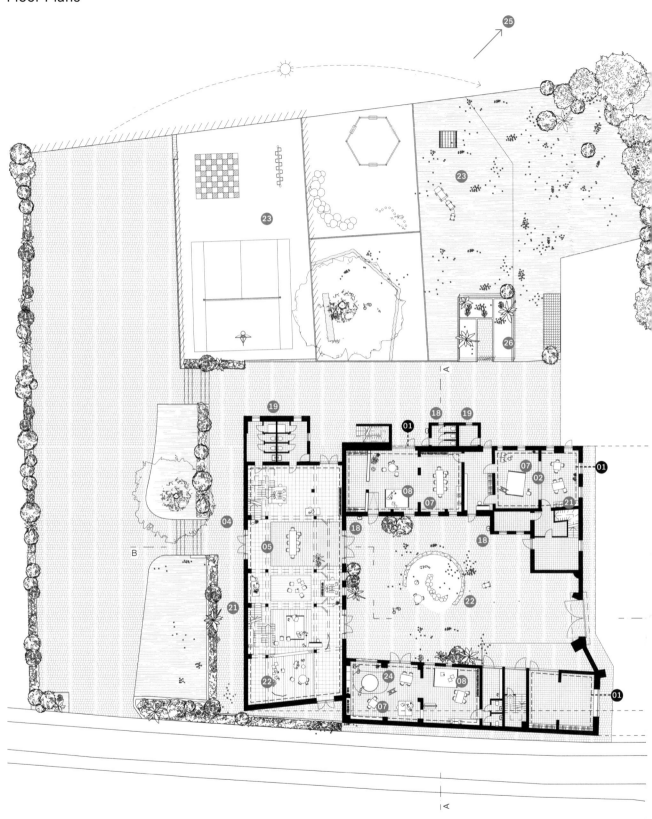

Ground Floor

0 1 3 5   10   20 m   1:400

In the original living quarters, a staircase and visitors' entrance connect with the first floor administrative office and the upper barn level which is once again a single space articulated by the rhythm of the compound truss structure. It has roof windows to the north looking over the courtyard and to the south over the garden. The space is used by the elementary age six- to nine-year-old children and has its own kitchen facilities and toilets within the space.

The garden and play areas to the south of the building extend down a hill with open fields beyond. At the lowest level of the garden is the pony enclosure and stable with two ponies. It is the children's responsibility to care for the ponies. At the higher level, immediately to the south of the buildings and across their entire extent, is a wide paved terrace with external water supply and trestle tables. This gives access to a ball court for various ball games and an outdoor giant chessboard. Adjacent to the ball court is an area for climbing frames. The remaining area consists of a soft grass-landscaped garden with areas for growing plants and for keeping smaller animals. The boundary to this area is marked by a line of potted Christmas trees which are cared for by the children and which are available for parents to rent for the Christmas period.

Pat. 03 ↗p. 54
Use of indigenous
materials ...

Pat. 22 ↗p. 102
Everyday gathering
spaces ...

Pat. 01 ↗p. 50
A hierarchy of
interconnected spaces ...

Pat. 03 ↗p. 54
Use of indigenous
materials ...

Pat. 07 ↗p. 66
Articulation of space
and form ...

Pat. 11 ↗p. 76
Use of the walls and building fabric for storage space

Pat. 12 ↗p. 78
Open storage and display
of learning materials

Pat. 15 ↗p. 84
Creation of window
seats ...

246

Pat. 23 ↗p. 104
Integration of spaces for
gross motor development…

Pat. 26 ↗p. 110
Earth stewardship…

Maria Montessori School, Coach House
Hampstead, London,
United Kingdom

Subject	Children's house	Total area	867 m²
Design	Carrick Howell and	Open area	767 m²
	Lawrence Architects,	Footprint area	100 m²
	Richard Partridge	Gross floor area	92 m²
Year	2015	Classrooms/Workshops	1/0
Climate	Temperate zone	Number of students	22

The Maria Montessori School in Hampstead is one of five schools belonging to the Maria Montessori Institute. The Institute is one of the world's foremost Montessori teacher training organisations and is affiliated to the Association Montessori Internationale. The Maria Montessori Institute was founded as the Maria Montessori Training Organisation in London in the late 1950s by Mario Montessori, Maria Montessori's son.

Once the home to the training organisation, as well as the school, the five-storey building now houses just the Montessori school with two classrooms for three- to six-year-olds and one classroom each for age groups six to nine and nine to twelve. It is a prominent Victorian red-brick building with a generous garden, and was built by Arts and Crafts architect William Willett in 1886.

Whilst most of the school is within the adapted rooms of the main house, one Children's House classroom is largely purpose-designed in the converted and extended coach house in the garden of the main house. The project was undertaken in two phases by architects Carrick, Howell and Lawrence in collaboration with Richard Partridge. It was Richard Partridge who was responsible for the most intense and complex work in the second phase, which was completed in 2015.

The project is very small in scale, amounting to a built floor area of only 92 square metres. However, to a large extent it was an experiment in incorporating the developing spectrum of *Montessori Patterns* and can be seen as a test of them. Whilst having only a total of 92 square metres, the building has five different floor levels and access to the outside in three locations. Other than bay window doors to the outside and doors to the toilets, it has no doors. Pats. 01/06

The original coach house was constructed at the same time as the house in a smooth red brick. The new bay window is lead-covered and the bay windows are timber. Internally, the mezzanine floor is constructed from Douglas fir double joists and furniture-grade solid birch plywood. The building is heated by underfloor heating within the concrete screed and the floor covering is oak-veneered engineered board. Oak treads match the floor. The masonry walls are principally brick with a painted finish and bespoke solid birch ply shelving units and inserted in the masonry structure. The roof to the extension is a heavily insulated flat roof with a growing medium for sedum. A lead-covered concealed and cantilevered gutter runs the length of the extension forming the visible roofline on the garden side.

The existing coach house contains a mezzanine level within the double-height space with steps up to the upper level and internally down to the base floor level, which extends into the extension, through a small kitchen and then down steps to a lower garden level. The height of the extension was restricted to keep it unobtrusive to neighbours and it has a sedum green roof. The entrance level around the coach house has been arranged as a veranda with broad amphitheatre steps down to the garden level. Pats. 02/07/22

The bay window and entrance level doors are arranged to open out onto the veranda in good weather to provide an inside/outside workspace. Internally, the bay window forms the practical life area and it has its own water supply and sink. Pats. 05/08/18/20

The Children's House, which is designed for three- to six-year-olds, is entirely self-contained with toilets for both children and adults. A child-height kitchen is situated in the connecting space between the existing coach house and the new extension, and leads down four steps into a sensorial and cultural space which in turn connects via six further steps down to a maths and language space. See-through, double-sided shelving separates the sensorial and cultural area from the maths and language area. Pats. 12/13/19/21

The sensorial and cultural space has a bay window seat that opens onto the deck, and coloured glass windows at high and low levels, which face south and thus generate constantly changing patterns of streaming sunlight. Clerestory windows provide high-level daylight. Pats. 07/11/15/16

The maths and language space has a sill at garden level and below this internally the deep wall accommodates a 5 metre run of accessible shelving specially designed to accommodate the educational materials relevant to the space. The windows open onto the garden and the sill is itself a step up to the garden level. Pats. 11/24

The back wall to the building is on the north side and is also the garden wall separating the adjoining property; it is designed as a deep wall containing four alcoves of open shelves. Pat. 11

The overall complexity of the spaces means that no focus of reflected sound waves arises, and this makes for a very benign and calm sound environment. The interplay of the various spaces and levels allows for a visual connectedness but in a way which allows observation without intrusion, and offers children places of relative seclusion. Pats. 13/14

The existing garden of the school is divided into six principal areas. A cultivated garden for growing vegetables and plants, an animal area for rabbits and guinea pigs, a climbing area, a general activities and games area and a grassed garden with seating and a small tarmac area with a basketball hoop; this serves also as a side entrance for parents. Pats. 23/25

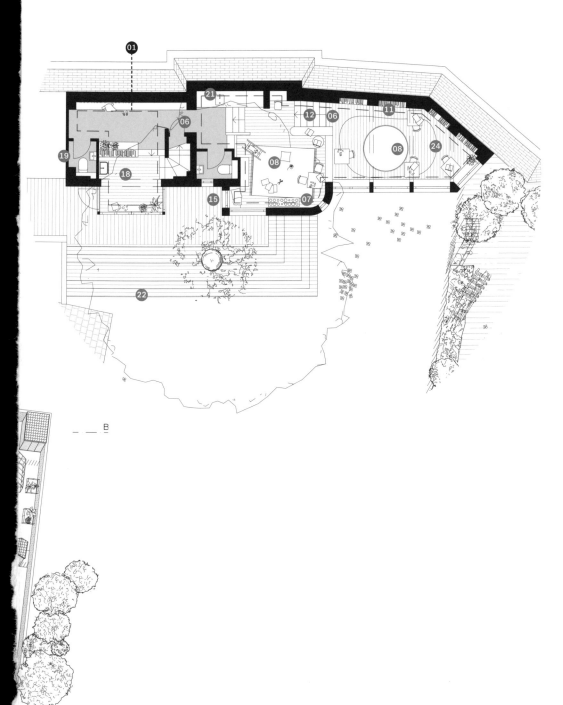

B

0 1   3   5   10 m   1:200

Sections

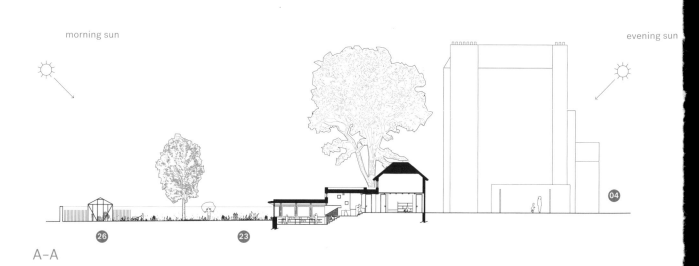

morning sun   evening sun

04

26   23

A–A

morning sun

B–B

0 1 3 5   10   20 m   1:400

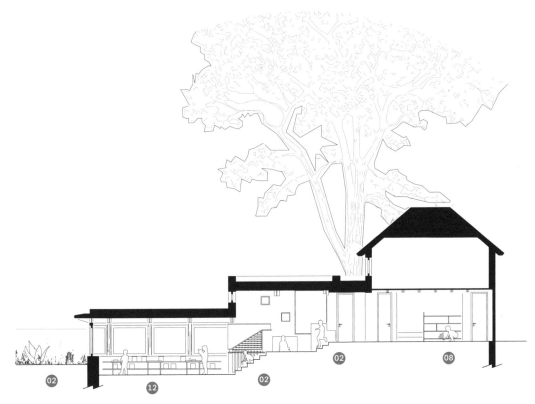

0 1   3   5   10 m   1:200

Floor Plan

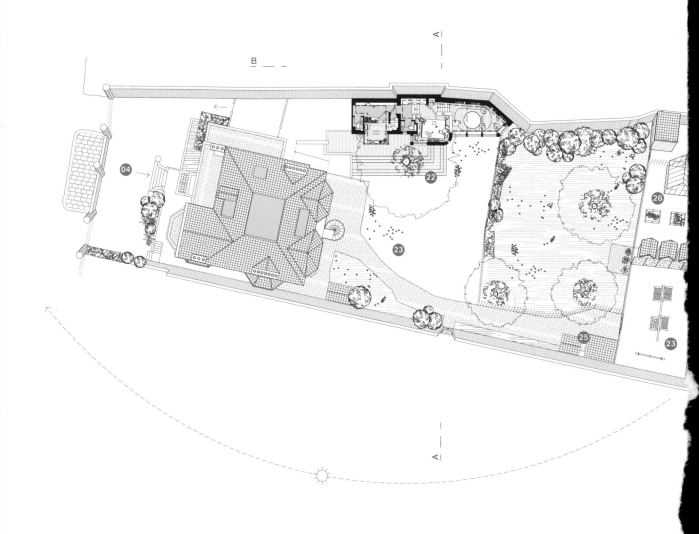

0 1 3 5   10   20 m   1:400

Pat. 04 ↗p. 58
Orientation of the
entrance …

Pat. 05 ↗p. 60
Connecting function of
the greeting space …

Pat. 02 ↗p. 52
Different heights for floors
and ceilings ...

Pat. 03 ↗p. 54
Use of indigenous
materials ...

Pat. 20 ↗p. 96
Transitional spaces be-
tween inside and outside ...

Pat. 22 ↗p. 102
Everyday gathering
spaces ...

Pat. 23 ↗p. 104
Integration of spaces for
gross motor development ...

Pat. 02 ↗p. 52
Different heights for floors
and ceilings ...

Pat. 03 ↗p. 54
Use of indigenous
materials ...

Pat. 20 ↗p. 96
Transitional spaces be-
tween inside and outside ...

Pat. 03 ↗p. 54
Use of indigenous
materials …

Pat. 23 ↗p. 104
Integration of spaces for
gross motor development …

The Montessori Place
East Sussex, United Kingdom

Subject	Primary school, secondary school, Children's House	Total area	47,197 m²
		Open area	46,206 m²
Design	Paul Pillai, Rob Gueterbock	Footprint area	991 m²
Year	2017	Gross floor area	880 m²
Climate	Temperate zone	Classrooms/Workshops	5/1
		Number of students	150

Pat. 18 ↗p. 92
Meaningful access
to water...

Pat. 25 ↗p. 108
School and grounds
as a habitat for animals
and plants

The Montessori Place has been developed in an existing residential building forming the northerly, long side, of a walled kitchen garden formerly within the grounds of a Victorian house built circa 1875 called 'The Whyly'. For a time the house was used as a religious centre for which the extended residential accommodation, now forming the school, was built. The grounds include woods to the north of the site, the walled garden, tennis courts to the south of the walled garden and further woods to the south up to a boundary with farmland. The situation is therefore very rural.

Eason's Green is the second site to be developed by the Montessori Place, the first being in a residential building in Hove. The first location is a Children's House for three- to six-year-old children and the site at Eason's Green is designed to cater for expansion into elementary and young adult age groups. The young adult age children are resident from Monday to Friday on the Eason's Green site.

The upper level of the building forms the children's living accommodation, the lower level accommodates the six to nine and nine to twelve age groups and the classroom for twelve to fifteen year olds. A second building, a barn, has been specially constructed to accommodate a Children's House for three to six year olds at the west end of the site and at right angles to the main building.

The form of the main building is very simple; it is long and low, and its ridge is constructed on the old garden wall, which makes for very difficult internal spatial division. Internally, the old wall is perforated at both upper and lower levels to allow access from side to side. The upper level rooms are naturally lit through a total of forty-eight dormer windows, twenty-four on each roof plane.

The east end of the main building is occupied by the school and the west end is residential accommodation for staff. The upper level at the east end consists of both boys' and girls' shared living/dormitory bedrooms and a corridor giving access to individual bedrooms and shared bathrooms.

The ground floor is entered by the older children on the central axis from a fenced garden on the north side; the greeting space opens directly onto the young adults' common area which looks out over the walled garden on its central axis. A staircase gives direct axis to the individual bedrooms above. The younger elementary age children enter through a second lobby space towards the east end of the building on the north side. The elementary and young adult classrooms are connected through a shared dining room which opens out onto the walled garden.

A broad footpath along the south-facing facade of the building has been created, and a small raised terrace opens into a back entrance and boot room. An external porcelain sink is fixed beside the back door. [Pat.18]

A centrally sited but derelict pond has been excavated by the children in the walled garden and it, in effect, divides the garden into formal quadrants. The southeast quadrant includes a poly-tunnel and the quadrant surrounding the poly-tunnel is cultivated with vegetables for consumption and includes an enclosure for ducks. The remainder of the garden is laid to grass. [Pat. 25]

One of the defining elements of the school is the workshop. It is well equipped, and the children are engaged in manufacturing real and useful things for enterprise around the school, in the kitchen garden and the surrounding landscape. The produce from the kitchen garden is used in the school and some crops are sold. The school has beehives and the children harvest the honey. This productive enterprise serves as a vehicle for an immense range of academic work in the school involving botany, biology, chemistry, physics, mathematics, language, economics, history, geography and anthropology. The focus of research on real life in this way is highly motivating. Pats. 25/26/27

The former tennis courts have been brought back into use and now constitute a ball court, including basketball hoops and football goal posts. The second building on the site takes the form of an aisled barn clad with cedar shiplap boards. It has a large picture window on the central axis with the sill as a window seat at its south end looking onto the landscape. It is entered from the fenced garden on the north side of the main school building and it has its own fenced garden with climbing equipment. Pats. 15/23

The barn is a stand-alone Children's House for the three-to-six years age group and the children have full access to the rest of the school and gardens. Pat. 09

The central aisle of the barn includes generous space for Walking on the Line. The east aisle opens onto a small external deck as a workplace which also gives secondary access to the fenced garden. The west aisle has three picture windows looking over the main access garden. The toilets are accessed from the main space. Pat. 19

The aisles are laid out with low-level accessible storage for the Montessori materials. A variety of individual desks and chairs are laid out and are small enough for the children to rearrange independently; these include small-scale upholstered chairs along with side tables for reading. Spotlights installed in the ceilings supplement low-level individual domestic-scale task lighting. Pats. 17/28

The internal floor is oak parquet over underfloor heating forming a comfortable workplace. The energy requirements for the barn are served by extensive ranges of photovoltaic panels fitted above clay tiles on both the east- and west-facing roof slopes. Pat. 3

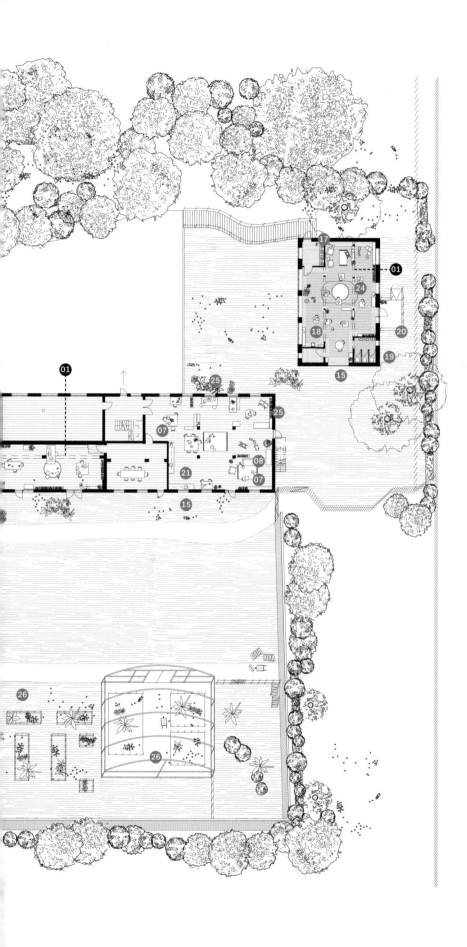

Sections

A–A

morning sun

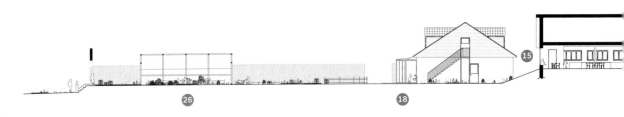

B–B

0 1 3 5   10   20 m   1:400

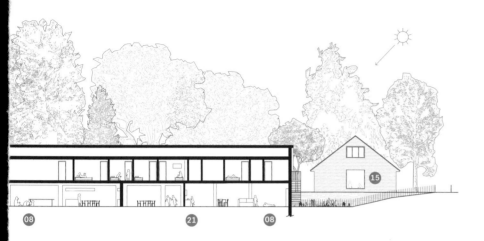

08   21   08   15

evening sun

07   23

Floor Plan

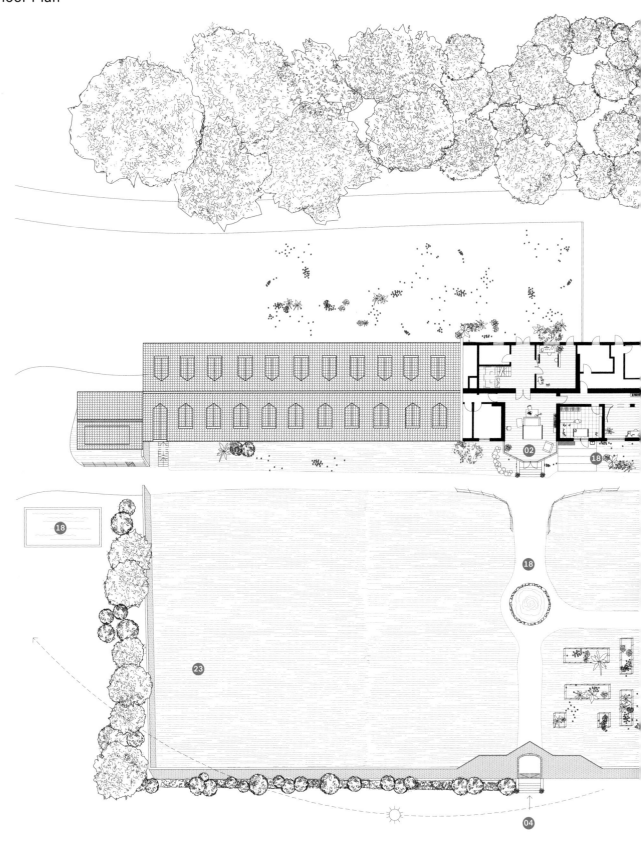

0 1 3 5   10   20 m   1:400

Pat. 03 ↗p. 54
Use of indigenous
materials …

Pat. 04 ↗p. 58
Orientation of the
entrance …

Pat. 18 ↗p. 92
Meaningful access
to water …

Pat. 03 ↗ p. 54
Use of indigenous
materials ...

Pat. 15 ↗ p. 84
Creation of window
seats ...

Pat. 01 ↗ p. 50
A hierarchy of
interconnected spaces...

Pat. 06 ↗ p. 62
Avoidance of doors...

Pat. 07 ↗ p. 66
Articulation of space
and form...

Pat. 27 ↗ p. 112
Children's workshop …

Pat. 26 ↗ p. 118
Earth stewardship …

BIBLIOGRAPHY

Alexander, Christopher W.; Ishikawa, Sara; Silverstein, Murray: *A Pattern Language*. Oxford 1977

Baker, Kay: *The Second Plane of Development (6–12 years)*. In: *AMI Journal 2017–2018 Double Issue*. Amsterdam 2018

Doesburg, Theo van: *De Stijl*, Vol.1–1. Delft 1917

Gross, Karl: *The Play of Man*. New York 1901

Haines, Annette: *Absorbent Mind Update – Research Sheds New Light on Montessori Theory*. In: Kahn, David: *NAMTA Journal*, Vol.18–2. Cleveland Heights 1993

Haines, Annette: *Glossary of Montessori Terms, 2001* (2001). In: *AMI Journal 2017–2018 Double Issue*. Amsterdam 2018

Hales, Linda: *A Lesson in Simple but Edifying Architecture*. In: *Washington Post 29 January 2005*. Online under http://washingtonpost.com/wp-dyn/articles/A46072-2005Jan28.html

Hellbrügge, Theodor. *Early Social Development*. In Kahn, David: *The NAMTA Quarterly*, Vol.4–3. Cleveland Heights 1979

Hertzberger, Herman: *Space and Learning*. Rotterdam 2008

James, William: *Psychology – Briefer Course* (1892). Reprint Notre Dame 1985

Jansen, Cilly: *Archief Grimmon*. https://adgrimmon.nl/info/ 2022

Kramer, Rita: *Maria Montessori: A Biography*. New York 1976

Montessori, Carolina: *Maria Montessori Sails to America: A Private Diary, 1913*: Laren 2013

Montessori, Maria: *Il Metodo della Pedagogia Scientifica applicato all'educazione infantile nelle Casa dei Bambini* (1909). Published in English as: *The Montessori Method*. New York 1912

Montessori, Maria: *Dr. Montessori's Own Handbook*. London 1914

Montessori, Maria: *The Absorbent Mind* (1949); *La mente del bambino – Mente assorbente* (1952). English translation by Clermont C., New York 1967

Montessori, Maria: *L'auto-educazione nelle scuole elementari – Parte II* (1916). Published in English as: *The Advanced Montessori Method II*. New York 1989

Montessori, Mario M.: In: *Vijftig jaar Amsterdamse Montessorischool, 1917–1967*. Amsterdam 1967

Montessori, Mario M: *The Human Tendencies and Montessori Education* (1956). Amsterdam 2018

Müller, Thomas; Schneider, Romana: *Montessori. Lehrmaterialien 1913–1935, Möbel und Architektur. Teaching Material 1913–1935, Furniture and Architecture*. Munich 2002

Osterkorn, Jon: *Socialization and the Development of Self Concept*. In: Kahn, David: *The NAMTA Quarterly*, Vol.5–3. Cleveland Heights 1980

Peller-Roubiczek, Lili; Schuster, Franz: *Ein "Haus der Kinder"*. Circa 1931. Online under http://eichelberger.at/dokumente/84-haus-der-kinder-wien-1-rudolf-splatz

Robson, David: *Geoffrey Bawa—The Complete Works*. London 2002

Schwarz-Hierl, Elisabeth (1923). In: Müller, Thomas; Schneider, Romana: *Montessori. Lehrnmaterialien 1913–1935, Möbel und Architektur. Teaching Material 1913–1935, Furniture and Architecture*. Munich 2002.

Sellon, Emily; Weber, Renée: *Theosophy and the Theosophical Society*. In: Faivre, Antoine; Needleman, Jacob: *Modern Esoteric Spirituality. World Spirituality*, Vol.21. New York 1992

Sidy, Victor: *Lessons from Taliesin West – NAMTA's Montessori Architecture Symposium*. In: Kahn, David (editor): *NAMTA Journal*, Vol.30–2. Burton 2005

Srinivasan, Prasanna; Ramachandran, Rukmini; Srinavasan, Vasumuthi; Roche, Hadrien; Venkatesan, Govind: *Montessori in India – 70 Years*. Chennai 2009. Pre-reading material for 2016 Educateurs sans Frontières assembly in Hyderabad, India

Standing, Edwin M.: *Maria Montessori – Her Life and Work*. New York 1957

Weiner, Edmund; Simpson, John: *The Compact Oxford English Dictionary, Second Edition*. Oxford 1991

Wilson, Carolie E.: *Montessori in India: A Study of the Application of her Method in a Developing Country*. Sydney 1987

IMPRINT

Initiative and realisation
Arthur Waser Foundation, Lucerne
Association Montessori Internationale, Amsterdam

Authors
Benjamin Stæhli
Steve Lawrence

Historical research
Carolina Montessori
Joke Verheul

Editorial support
David Keller
Judith Orion
Marco Meier
Monika Arnold
Konstantin Reiher
Lynne Lawrence
Soraya Lallani

Copyediting
Samantha Phillips

Proofreading
Colette Forder

Design
Nadine Wüthrich

Photographs
Benjamin Stæhli

Plan drawings
Bahoz Issa
Sandra Barmettler
Yannick Fortiguerra

Lithography
Marjeta Morinc

Printing
Druckerei Odermatt AG, Dallenwil

© 2023 Arthur Waser Foundation, Lucerne, Association Montessori Internationale, Amsterdam, and Park Books AG, Zurich

© for the texts:
the authors
© for the images:
see image credits

Park Books
Niederdorfstrasse 54
8001 Zurich
Switzerland
www.park-books.com

Park Books is being supported by the Federal Office of Culture with a general subsidy for the years 2021–2024.

ISBN
978-3-03860-315-3